What others are saying about *The Importance of Being Human*

With his out-of-the-box thinking, Dr. Glenn challenges the often-unconscious assumptions about life and our purpose in being here. He presents a stimulating perspective that breathes life into our understanding of relationships with ourselves, our Designer, and each other. Highly recommended!
—*Lana Seale, physical therapist and missionary*

This book is a "life preserver" for our time. Every day the world seems to be sinking in a quicksand of selfishness, corruption and absurdity; we need help. Through this book Dr. Strauss extends his hand, experience, and insight to show us a better way. With a fresh perspective on "living according to our design," he opens our eyes to see the myths pervading the culture around us, how they're impacting us, and what we can do about it. We highly recommend reading this book for a new look at ways to change your life—for the better!
—*Brian and Pauline Harris, engineer and marketing specialist*

This book provides an entire training manual for the development of human character, complete with operating instructions!
—*Jonathan Strauss, son*

This book is intriguing, thought-provoking, and powerful. If you're looking to recharge and refocus your faith, you'll be compelled to make some interesting adjustments in your walk with Christ. Allow yourself the time to grow and experience some old as well as some exciting new ways to redeem the days ahead.
—*Steve Morris, author and coach*

The Importance of Being Human explores the wisdom behind God's Master Plan for His creation and the significance of each individual's role in that plan. If you have ever wondered What is my purpose? Does my life really matter? . . . read this book!
—*Karen Morris, educator*

Dr. Strauss steps up to fill a void in our lost and chaotic society. I am reminded of J. H. Merle d'Aubigné's opening in Chapter One of his first volume of the *History of the Reformation* where he says, "The enfeebled world was rocking on its base when Christianity appeared." Today we

continue to rock perilously on the sinking sand of our misunderstandings of the meaning of life. Glenn correctly identifies our existential challenge when he says, "The creation of meaning is my greatest responsibility and privilege as a human being." I recommend that we read Glenn's book and take another look at how we can create meaning with our lives. *The Importance of Being Human* brings us back to an understanding of how we must live as creatures made in the image of God to make faith more than a platitude.
—*John Hunter, theologian and missionary*

The Importance of Being Human leads us on an insightful and convicting journey out of the "cultural echo chamber" of political correctness and away from our toxic pursuit of significance, power, and prominence. Dr. Strauss helps us embrace the Wisdom of the Creator and by doing so, brings us back to the faith, hope, and love humanity so desperately needs today. I recommend this book for anyone who needs a refresher course in who we are as human beings.
—*Lindsey Gainer, educator and administrator*

Dr. Strauss's prescient warning about the current state of Western culture reminds us of what we need to do to deal with the directionless void our society has given us. His book analyzes common beliefs, which lead to emptiness in people's lives and confusion about what we are really designed for. With his years of experience and acquired wisdom, he gives practical advice for how to recognize the problems confronting us, and how to make right choices in line with how God created us.
—*Scott Line, businessman*

One of the most pressing questions of our day—though often unasked—is that of anthropology, what does it mean to be human? Here, Glenn invites you to ask that question and join him in reflecting on the complexity and beauty of our humanity. Read. Think. Change.
—*Dr. Randy Randall, author and Reverend*

"What an intriguing topic! Glenn takes us deep into the workings of our divine design. He clearly explains how it was compromised but encourages us with how it can be restored. He dives into these deep waters with godly wisdom & humor. If you want to live in the fullness of your divine design, this is the book for you."
—*Valerie Arnold, business owner*

The Importance of Being Human

Our design is just what this world needs!

Glenn Strauss, M.D.

The Importance of Being Human
© Copyright 2023 Glenn Strauss, M.D.
ISBN: 979-8-9872779-5-9

All Scripture quotations are from the King James Version of the Bible and are public domain.

All rights reserved. No part of this publication may be reproduced or transmitted in any form or by any means without written permission from the publisher.

Interior graphics and cover design: Marji Laine
Cover photo: Brian and Pauline Harris ©2023
Editing: Karen Steinmann

Published by:
Roaring Lambs Publishing
17110 Dallas Parkway, Suite 260
Dallas, TX 75248

Published in the United States of America.

CONTENTS

Dedication 7
Foreword..8
Preface 12
Introduction 14
Part 1: Remembering what it means to be human 19
   Chapter 1: How did we get here?..21
   Chapter 2: What have we become?...31
   Chapter 3: Let Wisdom be our guide.......................................39
   Chapter 4: The myth of individualism.....................................51
   Chapter 5: How healthy individuality inspires community......55
   Chapter 6: The myth that love is a feeling 63
   Chapter 7: How boundless love is created 71
   Chapter 8: The myth of finding meaning in our busy, compartmentalized lives...81
   Chapter 9: How our divine design creates meaning and significance..89
   Chapter 10: The myth of power in positive thinking................99
   Chapter 11: How hope fuels our lives 105
   Chapter 12" The big picture..109
Part 2: Remembering how to act like human beings 113
   Chapter 13: How to live by divine design..............................115
   Chapter 14: Expressing my divine design in using authority..123
   Chapter 15: Expressing my divine design through a life of dignity 131

Chapter 16: Expressing my divine design through a life of virtue 141

Chapter 17: How to be a creator of love and meaning 155

Part 3: Remembering the story of the Creator 175

Chapter 18: Our built-in capacity for faith 177

Chapter 19: Exploring what the Creator reveals about being human 187

Chapter 20: Receiving the spiritual enhancements offered by the Creator 199

Chapter 21: Learning to use your spiritual enhancements 213

Chapter 22: Our divine design is just what this world needs 221

Appendix 1: The Good News About Our World 226

Appendix 2: How to Start a Conversation that Grows a Community 238

Acknowledgments 245

About the Author 246

Dedication

This book is written for my family in the hope that they will find here a bit of me and a lot of Jesus.

The Path Home
By G.H. Strauss

There are myths that hold us captive,

Stories that set us free;

There are tasks that bring us home

To rest in what we're designed to be.

Broken pieces of creation,

Partial truths of our design;

As shadows transformed to living wholeness

In the Presence of Light Divine.

Glenn Strauss, M.D.

Foreword

Throughout my life as a doctor, I have tried to observe what it is that makes some colleagues highly effective, competent, and even wise when I so often feel overwhelmed and clueless. Paradoxically, these traits often don't line up well with what we might label as "intelligence." As a surgeon, I have worked with people who were head and shoulders above anyone else in the room in raw braininess and book learning. Yet these people often were not the ones I would want to care for me in a dire emergency. I am more trusting of another group of people who somehow just inherently know the right questions to ask. Often these people were the experienced LPN (licensed practical nurse), the junior resident who had, before medical school, done time as a medic in Vietnam, people whose background as a rancher or contractor had forced them to look at situations with a practical eye to discern exactly what the central issue was. These are the providers who ask: What do we need to do right now? What do we do next? How does this test result guide my next move? How do I make the system, even in horrendously resource-poor environments, work the best that it can to help this individual survive? It is the right questions that frame a rapid and effective response.

Of course, this same principle applies to many other areas of life as well. Our thinking as spiritual beings can be prone to getting bogged down in the weeds with controversy and minutia. The people who have helped me the most with life's biggest challenges always seem to know the right spiritual questions to ask. Talking about learning the answers to the Big Questions when we reach heaven, C.S. Lewis once said, "It's like the sound of a chuckle in the darkness, the sense that some shattering and disarming simplicity is the real answer." I want to be around people who hear the chuckle in the darkness. Getting to the place of these simple yet real answers all begins with posing correct questions. If I had to give an example of a master "question-asker" in the realm of spiritual truth, this would be Dr. Glenn Strauss.

Glenn and I have known each other for many years and have stumbled with each other through pain in our families' lives, our personal journeys, our desire to walk in a way that is pleasing to God. There have been many questions. I remember many evenings after long days of surgery on a hospital ship in some West African port, where Glenn and I would meet for "rail time." After dark, we would sneak up to the upper deck of the ship and kind of lean over the railing and just talk when no one else was around. This was our time to debrief the day, decompress, talk about our problems, and figure out how to keep moving anyway. Depending upon how bad things were, the question of the night might not be some fine point of theology, but rather, "Do you still believe in God?" Glenn is no slouch theologically. He really could think deeply about Arminian vs. Reformed theology or the derivation of a particular Greek verb.

The idea that he would even entertain a question like, "Do you still believe in God?" completely blew my mind. And yet, after facing unholy suffering among the poorest of the poor day after day, this was a really great thing to keep asking. Sometimes one or both of us needed to argue this existential question back to a place of stability. The answer would be the thing to get us out of the bunk the next morning. Glenn has always been great at asking the right question. One question I often spewed as we leaned out over dark space, eight decks above the foul water below, always tongue in cheek but not that far from reality, was "Why not just jump and end it all?" Then we would stare at each other, my foot balanced on top of the rail, and Glenn would always answer, "Good thought. You go first!"

Glenn Strauss, M.D.

Now, we live at a later point in our careers and lives, and the issues are different. We are both approaching retirement age, both survivors of big family challenges, both struggling to function inside bodies that are no longer under warranty, trying to make sense of life in an increasingly truth-less world. The most amazing thing about our friendship is that we have always spent our time talking about the Big Truths much more than the Dallas Cowboys. Now, rather than joining our peers in talking about IRAs versus annuities as the soundest investment strategies for retirement, Glenn is back at asking big questions. For the past year or so, he has kept hammering on the same one: "What does it mean to be human?" In the beginning, this just frustrated me. Don't talk to me about my being; tell me what to do! But Glenn's question is an amazing one.

We Christians talk all the time about "knowing God." We study God's attributes and muse on the "character of God." These are critical topics to grapple with, central to our understanding of where our spiritual worldview is grounded. But, at some point, we must also ask similar questions of ourselves as human beings.

Growing up in the Church, I felt required to never forget that being human was a bad thing. We are "totally depraved," "Hell-bound sinners," beings who have offended an almighty God so badly that He had to kill His own Son to make up for our mistakes. And yet God made us human. Our humanity is a precious example of His grace toward us. Our humanity may include a curse, but also informs how we look at the world, at God, at our lives. There is so much good stuff to marvel at and be continually astonished. This takes work to see, but as John Donne reminded us: "It behooves us to be astonished."

Life as a human does not come with an owner's manual. We must look at what we know about God, how He made us and then somehow infused himself into our being, and then we must come up with a way to live that reflects the answer to Glenn's question.

Whether or not we like it, being human is something we can't escape.

Join Glenn in his exploration of the meaning of being human, and hopefully you can find positive Truth that will steer you toward a place where you can know the absolute joy of being exactly what you were made to be, just like a sheep dog herding sheep. If you don't want to be human anymore, the only other option lies just over the railing. You go first.

—*Dr. Steven Arrowsmith, 2023*

Preface

I suspect many people would agree that our world has gone mad! I'm writing this preface post-COVID shutdown during an insane geopolitical war in Ukraine and an ideological war at home in the U.S.A. Just three years ago I was writing *Finding the Way* (2019, Kindle Books) as a reminder of some good news about a divine plan for creation and our design to be partners in this plan as human beings. The good news? Jesus, the promised Jewish Messiah, modeled a perfect human partnership with the Creator. By doing so, He became humanity's first truly qualified advocate and leader, inviting all people to trust Him as The Way out of our cycles of self-destruction and into freedom to truly love as He did. I showed that a life following Jesus revitalizes our capacity for critical thinking, decision making, planning, and loving other human beings. Yet today, despite our potential, it seems we still prefer self-destructive behavior.

We have certainly seen dark days in human history before. There are so many stains on our soul as a race. But now, striving to be more than we are designed to be, we are becoming far less. We are riding a wave of demands to rid ourselves of personal limitations only to be pulled into the dark waters of a fragmented society underneath. We remain almost completely unaware of the danger of toxic individualism that celebrates each step towards freedom to be whatever we want, rather than our God-given freedom to choose within our design limitations to be human beings. As a result, we are more concerned about our freedom to be free than about the cost of our choices! Businesses exploit our desire to be happy, governments our desire to live our dream. Health gurus and medical systems exploit our desire to be healthy, lawyers our desire for justice. And sad to say, spiritual leaders often exploit our desire for community. When was the last time you could just enjoy being human without fear of someone taking advantage?

There are certainly those who stand against these dangers. But their words are often drowned out by the intrusive messages of our culture and amplified in the distorted world of social media, political correctness, and entertainment. These messages are reinforced by pervasive and insidious cultural myths about who and what we are and verified by the illusion of "human progress" through technological advances. You may be among those who fear the threat of climate change or nuclear destruction, social disintegration, or global economic collapse. But collectively, we seem to overlook the threat of irreparable damage to our soul as a race—a threat to our basic wiring as human beings. We cannot seem to help but be drawn towards the "light" of progressive thinking no matter the cost.

I am one of those standing against these threats. I see all too well the destructive stories we believe about ourselves and would like an answer to the question of what is so important about being a member of the human race. I am convinced that we must rediscover and embrace the transformative invitation to be a part of the most incredible human project ever—the Creator's project to restore what is truly good about creation. But the partnership between the Creator and human beings only works when we accept our design, limitations and all! Wouldn't it be incredible to genuinely enjoy just being human? It is possible! I hope this encourages you to read on.

—*G.H. Strauss, M.D., 2023*

Glenn Strauss, M.D.

Introduction

A little about me

After 40 years of teaching and serving others as a surgeon and pastor in over thirty-six countries including my own, I continue to be amazed at how often I guess wrong about how things will turn out. Good intentions? Check. Good plan? Check. Good support? Check. Expected result? Not so much. The way my life unfolded seemed to raise lots of "why" questions.

Why do decent, hard-working parents like mine sometimes miss the most important things about their child's spiritual life? Why would a wonderful, fun-loving wife like mine have to deal with a debilitating disease during the most important years of her children's lives? Why would a good surgical career like mine demand loyalty rather than simply provide security for my family and healing for others? Why do churches and mission organizations sometimes make it so difficult to succeed in loving and serving others? It all comes back to the most fundamental of questions we all ask: Why don't things turn out the way they are supposed to?

I am sure you've had some serious "why" questions of your own. For me, the struggle has produced a journey of discovery about how life works. For some, this leads to fatalistic thinking and despair, but for me it has led to a life-long pursuit of Wisdom. I have accomplished many good things in my lifetime. I have successfully performed tens-of-thousands of life-changing operations, invented training solutions and trained dozens of surgeons who work in low-income countries, counseled dozens of couples and individuals, built churches, spoken and performed in front of thousands, written books, provided for a family, and loved my wife faithfully for almost fifty years now. But thankfully, the nagging "why" questions just would not go away. I say "thankfully" because it is these questions viewed through the lens of Wisdom that have given me perspective and led to a startling realization: Life is not about the importance of accomplishments or control; it's about the importance of being human!

My wife and I recently stopped and asked ourselves, "How did we make it through all that has happened the last fifty years!" All the surprising good we achieved, all the unexpected benefits we received, all the challenges and sorrows we were able to face together—all were the undeserved fruit of building a life together focused on the relentless pursuit of Wisdom in a relationship with Jesus.

We take no pride in it, but we do take great joy in knowing we are where we are because we chose to live life as His followers. We have had our share of pain and failure, but I am happy to say we have no regrets about this path. You can listen to me because I am well studied in theology, medicine, and psychology, or because I have years of success in counseling, training, and international development work. But I hope you will listen to me because I am sharing a perspective about a path in life that has changed me for the better and has changed others' lives as well. This is why I wrote this book. And this is why I think you should pay attention to what I have to say.

A little about this book

In this book I extend a challenge to do life guided by Wisdom, not by technology, science, or cultural trends. I believe this book provokes thought and asks questions you need to answer. It tells a story of humanity's potential, our Creator's design, and how each of our personal stories play into all of this. I hope you hear the passionate voice of a caring teacher urging and cajoling his students to be something more than they thought possible. But I also want you to hear the voice of a loving parent encouraging his children (and grandchildren in my case!) to keep pursuing Wisdom like a precious gift.

I must confess, the surgeon in me comes out quite a bit in this writing. In fact, this book is laid out using the general plan I use to train cataract surgeons. I start by laying a foundation about how things work, explaining interactions, misconceptions, and basic tools and how they work. I then progress to suggesting specific strategies that help optimize each individual's potential, focusing on the development of effective habits that can be continuously developed. Finally, I suggest what each person should consider as a framework to sustain a life of service and commitment to being their best.

What looked effortless when I did surgery required years of practice to learn how to respond to the complexity of each moment. It is a bit like learning to dance—you learn "steps," but the goal is to experience the beauty of a well-choreographed routine. This approach made my training different, and I think more successful than most other training programs that emphasized the "just do what I do" approach. In my view, other strategies never gave the trainees enough to truly master the art of surgery.

My goal is to teach you the art of doing life according to your essential design. I will take you through the foundations, specific techniques, and finally a model for immersion with the Master. I will divide the discussion into three main parts.

1. Remembering what it means to be human beings.

2. Remembering how to act like human beings.
3. Remembering the story of the Creator.

Part 1 is our foundations study. This groundwork is incredibly important to take you beyond imitating what you see others doing to mastery. We will consider our design as human beings—how we are wired, what we have become, and how we got here as a human family. I retell our story as human beings with a focus on how we keep moving towards our potential but failing to get there. I will discuss the cultural messages that hold us captive. I explore our incredible human design and its potential revealed by Wisdom.

In Part 2, I provide a reminder of how to act like human beings. I elaborate on wise habits that reinforce the functions of our human design and provide examples of important activities that can help us thrive as a human family.

Lastly, in Part 3, I remind us of the purposes of our divine design by exploring the story of the Creator. I have found no better model for the best in humanity than what I see in the person of Jesus. We will explore how the Creator used Wisdom to define His commitment to us as a human family. We will see how Jesus, the personification of Wisdom, shows us that we as human beings are just what the world needs to thrive. Whether you believe in Jesus as the divine-human revelation of the Creator or not, His story beckons us all to consider a new way to see ourselves as a part of a much larger picture.

I would not be surprised if you wonder whether all this really matters or not. The funny thing is, you won't know until you begin to explore the issues for yourself. In fact, it is the process of asking the questions, seeking the answers, and knocking on the doors of your own imagination that will provide the Wisdom to see the significance and the importance of being human.

Glenn Strauss, M.D.

I hope to share some of the Wisdom I have gained over the past 50 years of following Jesus and encourage a younger generation to reconsider the fundamental importance of being human. I hope it will challenge all generations to become agents of change. I pray that as you consider these ideas, you will question, discover, and come to delight in what you are as a human: an incredible being, created in the image of God. What could be more important than that!

Part 1

Remembering what it means to be human

Glenn Strauss, M.D.

Chapter 1

How did we get here?

Our world is in big trouble . . . and perhaps the biggest problem of all is that we don't have a clue how we got here! This book is a warning cry about the dangerous waters in which we swim as a human race, completely unaware of what lurks just beneath the surface. These words are an attempt to throw a life ring to all who are growing weary swimming in the currents of life just trying not to drown. How did we get here? Why are injustice, corruption, and discrimination ripping us apart? Why are dehumanizing conditions so commonplace that we hardly notice them anymore? And what can we do about it?

We begin by taking a close look at what we have become as a human family. In this first chapter, I offer an overview of our story. Sadly, I think the beginnings of the mess we are in now showed up early on, but we seemed to miss all the warning signs. We followed a path that has taken us further and further away from what it means to be human.

The exact details of our origin as a species are interesting but irrelevant to my argument. For the purposes of this book, I only insist that we, from the very beginning, started with and continue to possess a recognizable divine design. Somehow, with much the same DNA as our ancestors, as well as the same essential design, the human family evolved from a tiny population fighting for survival with crude tools and weapons to be eight billion strong. We started our journey as a small migratory family in Mesopotamia and ended up populating the planet. Whatever else our world has become, however many years it took us to get here, we face an inescapable truth about our current condition as human beings: We are what we are now largely because of our own choices.

With all due respect for those much smarter and more studied than I about this topic, I offer here the story that represents our collective choices as a human family. It is simplified to draw attention to a pattern of growth and self-destruction dating back to our earliest history. A look at our story seems a reasonable first step in considering what it means to be a human being now.

So it begins

Prior to 4000 BC in what is called the pre-"historic" era (that is, before any written history), the human population was quite small. Conditions were harsh, and we used stone, fire, bronze, and iron to create tools and weapons to survive. It is widely believed that this was a period of migration from Mesopotamia (the Fertile Crescent) to the rest of the world though the exact dating is uncertain.

At that time, it was all about survival of the fittest. Only a rudimentary social order was necessary for navigating the harsh conditions. Following a global environmental disaster known as "the Great Flood," there was a reboot of the human family starting over from a small group of survivors. In a strange twist, this disaster was probably what kept the human family from annihilating itself completely.

From this small group of survivors, another story of human growth and migration is told. The population rapidly increased and spread, yet unfortunately with much the same self-destructive pattern as before the Flood. But this time, one of the descendants of a Flood survivor, a Chaldean named Abraham, is drawn to a "promised land" in which his descendants (later renamed the Hebrews) would become a means of spreading blessing to the rest of humanity. These descendants are then trained extensively by their God to understand His unique nature and character as the Creator. They are also instructed about how their human design worked. They were given a set of simple operating instructions so that they could live within their human limitations while making the most of their own nature and character as human beings.

Their story is of interest to me because the focus is on the power and Wisdom of the Creator to provide what was needed for humanity to thrive in partnership with Him. The story of the children of Abraham was a story of hope for humanity. They were given the chance to learn how to work in harmony with each other, the Creator, and the world around them rather than depending on the tools and weapons of survival and domination that characterized the stories of the self-destructive tribes all around them.

Tragically, due to their miserable failures to follow the path of Wisdom that could have led to success, they were absorbed as slaves into the Egyptian culture. Rather than living in the "promised land" on the eastern shore of the Mediterranean, they lived in the region around the Nile River. Despite many gracious and even miraculous chances to recover what was lost, they ended up enslaved not just once but several times! They never learned to thrive and eventually were thrust into captivity in the Babylonian world.

Aren't we something

Between 4000 BCE and 476 CE, the human population was growing, especially in the northern Mediterranean region. Survival became easier. This ushered in the period called the "classical era." This is the age of philosophers like Aristotle and Plato, who focused on the power of our transcendent human potential to create the ultimate civilizations. The transcendental values of truth, beauty, and goodness were taught not only as ideals but as essential functions of our design. These ideals proved to be potent cultural influences resulting in discoveries in the natural world, beautiful art, and massive architectural accomplishments.

This was also the time during which Jesus of Nazareth lived. I will have much more to say about Him in Part 3 of this book. But for now, I would point out that His life and teaching as a Jewish rabbi reminded a small group of mostly uneducated followers living under the oppression of Roman rule about the potential of their design as human beings. They saw in Him a reminder of the best of humanity, and this ignited a memory of and passion for the Wisdom that had been offered to humanity by the Creator. Despite persecution, or perhaps because of it, the movement of followers of this Jewish Messiah rapidly grew across the known world, and with it, a type of Wisdom quite different than what was taught by the philosophers. By the mid-300s CE, Christianity as it came to be called was not only accepted but mandated by Constantine as the official religion of the Roman Empire. This set the stage for the political expansion of the Church as an institution but did little for the spread of the message of the new heavenly kingdom it proclaimed.

The classical period ends rather abruptly with the fall of the Roman Empire in 476 CE, resulting in loss of civil law and order and major disruption for the followers of Jesus. The world as a whole fell into chaos controlled only by brute force. Once again, the family of man was headed for dark times. All traces of Wisdom of any kind seemed to have disappeared.

It couldn't get much worse

The period following the classical era was all about religious political domination (Roman Catholic, Eastern Orthodox, and Islam) and feudalism. Between 476 CE and 1450 CE, the once incredible classical era civilizations had deteriorated into what is called the "Middle Ages." You have probably heard it referred to as the "dark ages" because so much of the history is missing. But it was dark days for human development as well. We know little of the details, but the time is marked by regression of humanity to a savagery reminiscent of prehistoric man fighting for survival. The divine design of man and the Wisdom that was apparent in the classical period seemed all but erased.

Even the once dynamic movement of those expanding the Kingdom of God deteriorated as the focus shifted from the simple mandate of Jesus to love, to the power of religious creeds to shape and dominate people and land. The Bible and Qur'an, arguably the most influential books of all time, were canonized during this time, but access to them was controlled by individuals enticed by their power to control the masses. The Islamic and Christian followers fought for domination of their book and paid an enormous human price for it.

The good news is that during this time there is evidence that there was always a remnant of Jesus followers who remembered what it meant to be human. These were the "saints and martyrs" who resisted the corruption and power struggles of the day and often gave their lives for it. It was a time when Wisdom had a high cost.

A glimmer of hope

It's not clear to me how the cycle of destructive behavior finally began to wane. Perhaps it was a growing weariness and resistance to inhumane conditions, or maybe a spark still flickering in those who remembered what it meant to be human. It could have been wider accessibility to the newly published and translated Bible, plus a new emphasis on discovery. Whatever the cause, complex change in conditions gradually moved us into what is called the "Renaissance." Between 1450 and 1750 the focus shifted from political and religious power to the power of individual creativity and the human mind. This time is often referred to as the

"Age of Enlightenment." We commonly associate it with the discoveries of Galileo and Leonardo da Vinci or seafaring explorers. Humanity gradually moved out of the dark ages of religious domination and feudal terror into a more "enlightened" social order and even some degree of religious reformation and freedom, which grew out of the Protestant Reformation movement. It seemed that our divine design and interest in Wisdom was awakening after a long period of darkness.

Our journey as a human family to "enlightenment" produced incredible benefit. Evidence-based knowledge and personal happiness gradually became far more important than the superstitions and religious dogma of the Medieval dark ages. The age of scientific inquiry had begun. Theoretically, it was not necessary to be a priest, a royal prince, or a member of a dominant tribe or caste to succeed. With the proper education, anyone could control their future. Christianity also spread as it came to be more tolerant of the new scientific theories, in fact incorporating some of the same scientific methods into its own study as a theological discipline.

Towards the end of this period, colonial Americans believed that together they could accomplish anything if they could escape religious and political oppression. The Enlightenment was the foundation for the American dream and what led to the formation of the world's first democratic government. America was the first nation to be based entirely on Enlightenment thinking as pointed out by Alexis de Tocqueville, a French historian of the early 1800s.

But the benefits of the Enlightenment—both scientifically and religiously—seemed to be associated with opportunity only available to a relatively small segment of the growing population around the world. The power of science became the tool of the elite. Only some of the world entered the "modern era." The majority of the world did not. Instead, there was increasing separation between those who could enjoy the benefits of the Enlightenment and those who could not. Science became a tool for oppression and war. Our human design was again failing to help us reach our potential as a human family.

Let's get down to business

The modern era between 1750 and 1945 first took shape as the Industrial Age got rolling on the wings of continued population increase and scientific discoveries. This era was associated with what could at best be called a "civilized" approach to world domination known as colonialism. Our divine design enabled us to create wealth, not just talk about philosophical ideals. Many quickly realized that the ability to create wealth also provided the opportunity to control it. More resources were needed to keep the industrial machine running smoothly. New discoveries drove new opportunities and more demand. This inevitably led to the exploitation of other humans and lands where valuable natural resources existed in abundance. The developed world justified their exploitation by believing scientific empiricism would crank out the solutions to solve the world's problems . . . eventually.

The Christian impact in the developed world didn't help much either. Instead of holding society accountable to ethical standards, religion became ever more fragmented as denominations and revivalism staked claims to people and land. Religion became a primary tool for the Nazi agenda (though it was resisted by theologians like Dietrich Bonhoeffer). In the end, the powers that wanted to control the resources could not control themselves. This resulted in tragic conflict between tribes and nations, haves and have nots, even religious denominations. Power was more important than truth or ethical standards.

It's no surprise that this would produce catastrophic world war. Instead of using our industriousness to create prosperity and freedom for all, we used it to build weapons of oppression and domination. We were confronted as a human family with the reality of limited resources and responded with cruel brutality rather than Wisdom. Though the world war finally ended, the world map was held together with fragile treaties and agreements still focused on protecting wealth. The industrial war engine was slowly redirected to rebuilding the future, turning ever more fervently to the hope that technology could now be the driver of our success since brute strength could not. It seems that Wisdom was an unnecessary or, at best, a questionable guide in the face of the "objective" truth of Science. Wisdom and science grew further and further apart. The ideological war was far from over.

The "I's" have it

This brings us to the mid-1900s and the beginnings of the information age. The cost of colonialism became unsustainable as the global population exploded. The world map was constantly changing. Market forces were redefining the human landscape.

Advances in science and information became our obsession. Democratizing information created a "me first" world. Technological advances now define social, economic, and political growth rather than improvement in human character.

Driven, it seems, by a persistent belief in the enlightenment story that our minds could save us, our hearts have grown colder towards spiritual things and Wisdom has become less relevant or not even tolerated in the public forum. Churches adopted more studied methods of marketing their attractive distinctives rather than promoting unity in spiritual essentials. These days, there is arguably more dogma about political agenda and the literal meaning of specific hot button words than teaching about life and Wisdom. Theology, science, and social media have become the battleground for proving who is in and who is out.

It's certainly not all bad. Not all have followed these trends. But it begs the question: What happened to the original and more complete picture of our divine design? What happened to Wisdom? Who is carrying the ball for the human race now? I believe we can answer these questions by zooming in for a closer look at what we have become as a human family.

Chapter 2

What have we become?

Because life was so much better after the dark ages, perhaps we just did not see the trouble coming. We never stopped to ask what we were becoming as a human family on our journey from the caves to the high-tech world. For those who grew up with the incredible advances of science and technology, it just makes sense that life is better because we are smarter and more educated than ever before. We believe science and technology have not just made life better—they have made us better. After all, this was the promise of the Enlightenment. We are products of Enlightenment-based thinking about ourselves and our place in the world. Deeply embedded within us is the idea that our progress as the human race is measured by our advances in knowledge and technology. Maybe this is why we don't look beyond our advances to what we are becoming.

What have we become?

What we failed to account for was the possibility that the incredible advances could actually be hiding something dangerous.

Glenn Strauss, M.D.

As the empirical sciences and machines come to dominate our world, we cannot or perhaps do not want to see what is happening. We will not look behind the curtain as humanity begins to whither, not in an apocalyptic sense, but in more subtle ways. Ever-increasing environmental, sociological, spiritual, and anthropological damage have been hiding in plain sight, comfortably integrated with the conveniences we developed. We don't hesitate to pollute our world as long as we have plastic water bottles; we don't worry about the damage done to young people as long as we can market our products however we want to whomever we want; we don't stop and think about the increase in violence as long as we get to play our violent video games. We have gradually become cogs in the very machine we created. In our efforts to become more independent of our limitations, we have become less human in profound ways.

There is no denying the unexpected consequences of our "success" around us everywhere. Financial and social injustice are endemic. Expressions of hatred and violence are everyday occurrences. Nations continue to rise against nations with unconscionable loss and even genocide. Trash is filling our air and our world. It is fair to say that living conditions are indeed better than a century ago, at least in the developed world. We are smarter than ever. But if how things are now signify that knowledge and technology are the key to our "success" as human beings, I would say something is terribly wrong with how we define success! There is no question that knowledge and technology can make us feel smart, comfortable, and secure. But when we look around us, can we really claim to be "successful"? Maybe not.

Just how bad is it?

Truthfully, our problems only continue to get worse. Today in the Information Age we are not so much cogs in the machine as data points in the computer. In this digital version of the Industrial Age everything about what we do is measured, stored, and analyzed for efficiency and productivity. What we don't see is that the original promise of knowledge giving us the power to control our lives has taken a dark turn. The sheer volume of information is increasing far faster than we can process it. We have become slaves to the information we generate. Knowledge controls us.

In a final twist to the story of our pursuit of advancements, we are now seeing an erosion of confidence in anything absolute. With the gradual loss of any way of "knowing" except through physical evidence, our spiritual capacity for faith has atrophied. It's no surprise that as the promise of the Enlightenment fades, our individual opinions and experiences have become the dominant way of deciding what is true. We now fully expect the scientific "facts" to change. If you don't like what your doctor says today, just wait till tomorrow for something new. Go to a website that tells you what you want to hear. Artificial intelligence engines churn out replicas of our thinking and creativity based on massive pools of what we already know or what others want us to believe.

You must wonder sometimes, why are there so many "proven" answers to personal health and happiness? And how is it that businesses and governments so easily exploit our desire to be happy? Health gurus and medical systems exploit our desire to be healthy. Lawyers exploit our desire to "win." And well-meaning or not, spiritual leaders sometimes exploit our desire to belong. Is this the price we must pay for "advancing" as human beings?

These days, empirical knowledge is constantly undermined with conspiracy theories, "fake news," infotainment (entertaining ourselves with new and more dramatic "facts"), popular trends, and revisionist history. Personal experience rather than evidence is gradually becoming the basis for faith and facts. What else can we trust, right?

Instead of gathering information, we create our own. More convinced than ever of our ability to progress as individuals, the religion of empiricism is being replaced by the religion of individualism as we shall discuss in Chapter 4. My point here is that we have learned to trust no one but ourselves. Achieving personal success by advancement of knowledge and technology has left the developed world dehumanized, narcissistic, and disempowered. Quite the opposite of what we want to believe about ourselves.

Our advancement in technology and knowledge itself is good, but this advancement has produced a monstrous problem that more information and better technology cannot resolve. We believe the evolutionary story that we have become the most powerful and successful creatures on the planet because of what we have achieved, not because of how we live. Consequently, we do not see the reality of what we have become. We simply cannot afford to believe it's really all that bad.

Why can't we see it?

I invite you to just take a step back with me and breathe as we continue this line of reasoning. Are we finally to the point where we can't see the consequences of our progress? Are our achievements only producing delusions of grandeur and actually keeping us from enjoying our potential and our importance as human beings? My hope is to expose the old Enlightenment story of better living through science as a failed promise and convince you that we are designed for so much more.

It's not that we lack intelligence—quite the opposite. We are smart enough to build a narrative that supports what we want. Modern cultural myths have gradually crept in to prop up our stubborn insistence that we are better people than a century ago. I know the idea of a "myth" sounds a bit archaic, but I am using the term here to describe a pervasive, cultural belief based only on a tradition. The powerful myths of our time are rooted in the grandiose Enlightenment belief that we can think our way to a better future. These beliefs define our Western culture and modern "political correctness." As a result, we only see the advantages in technological advances with little concern for the problems they cause.

We as the human family are afraid of giving up the Enlightenment story and our modern cultural myths because we might have to give up more than we will get. We use these myths to tell ourselves we are okay and making progress. And by "we" I mean all of us who are beneficiaries of modern "progress," not a few conspirators somewhere trying to control us.

So, what do our modern myths look like? No one is out announcing them. There are no books of modern mythology that I can find. They are more subtle than that. For example, there is the belief that individualism can set us free. We hear this myth in how we tell our news stories and who our heroes are. Or maybe the belief that love is a feeling we all deserve no matter the cost. Just look at the sheer number of romantic novel book titles today. Maybe you truly believe that you will find meaning in your possessions or that there is power in positive thinking.

I am sure every reader will recognize the pervasiveness of these ideologies in our culture. You might struggle with the idea that they might actually be myths! In fact, there is a good chance you might already feel a little on the defensive right now! We really think these ideas are true. But hear me out on this. Surely you will agree that something is wrong and be willing to accept the possibility that our beloved ideals might be tragic mistakes—simply cultural-based beliefs. We need not accept a path paved with modern myths which, I believe, are at the root of our failure to progress as human beings despite our advancement in so many other ways. These are "the myths that hold us captive" because they go against the very essence of what it means to be human.

There is a path home

Armed with a willingness to expose the myths and a little out-of-the-box thinking, I believe we can still remember the importance of being human. That's the main theme of this book. It's time to wake up and see that technology and knowledge are not the problem—but that the myths we believe about ourselves are. When we fail to acknowledge our design, we risk damaging our humanity.

Before jumping into a full discussion of these myths, we must take one small detour to say a little more about what I mean by "divine design." The path home I describe in this book begins with acknowledging the uniqueness of human beings within the cosmos. We are different from any other animal. We're not just unique as individuals within the human race; our whole race is unique among animals. I believe this uniqueness strongly suggests a divine Designer. The truth that such a Designer exists can of course be debated and often is. Though you may reject the idea out of hand, if you will grant me the possibility that there is an intentional design (regardless of exactly how it happened), we can continue our journey. In the process, you may discover that our design itself is actually proof enough of a Designer.

For now, we begin by looking at what I believe is our primary resource for the journey—Wisdom. It has always been part of our story as human beings. As a concept it goes back as far as anything we know of, and I believe I can show it has considerable modern application. We will use the next chapter to refresh and refine our thinking about the concept of Wisdom.

Glenn Strauss, M.D.

Chapter 3

Let Wisdom be our guide

There's nothing wrong with knowledge and technology. I have spent most of my career teaching. Education of the mind is a foundation for development. And I love technology. I strongly believe we are designed to learn, grow, and discover new things. I myself have been significantly involved in the development of high-tech virtual reality training tools, taught advanced surgical skills, and trained hundreds of trainers. There is nothing intrinsically wrong with empirical science. It has unlocked many doors and helped make our world a better place in many ways.

The problem is, we are not purely empirical beings. We are not just a mind that needs to be educated and bodies that need to be exercised. I believe we also have a soul—a part of us that transcends the physical. Compelling evidence exists, both from a philosophical point of view and the study of near-death experiences, that this is true. Consider the fact that you somehow know that the body of a deceased loved one is just a shell. Or that you may have experienced times when your spirit is broken, not just your emotions. We know there is more to life than flesh and bones.

The truth is, empirical science and technology can help us only so much with these transcendent realities. Using science and technology to make sense of our soul is like using instructions for operating a boat to fly an airplane. We need something that better aligns with all aspects of our human design, not just certain parts of it. We need a guide to the transcendence of being human.

This brings us to one of the main themes of this book: Wisdom, though ancient in its origin, was and still is the best guide for understanding how our divine design works and how to use it properly. Far from being some mystical source of hidden knowledge, I believe Wisdom is just the guide we need to help us expose the confusing myths of our culture and direct us in the skills we need for thriving as human beings. Wisdom can be our guide to the transcendence and importance of being human.

It would be wonderful if Wisdom were simply an intellectual pursuit—something we can pass on to our children like a nice piece of furniture. But in reality, Wisdom does not come from the self-help aisle or even the wise words of a grandparent. (I am happily thinking about my own grandchildren here!) So where does it come from?

Why Wisdom works

A little history shows us two options to consider as the source of Wisdom. Nowhere is the source of Wisdom more eloquently portrayed than in the story of King Solomon who lived about 1000 BCE. Son of the already successful King David, Solomon is given the opportunity to ask for anything from God. What does he ask for? He asks God for something surprising—the gift of Wisdom. Why would he ask for something so abstract? Today we might think, "If the genie in the bottle gives you a wish, why waste it on wisdom?"

The reason is, Solomon had a worldview in which Wisdom originated with the God of his ancestor, Abraham. He believed it was Wisdom that brought order to all of creation in the beginning of the human story. He believed that Wisdom was the ultimate guide in dealing with the complexity of human nature. In a way, he believed God was offering him the same resource He used to create human beings and build the world! He only needed to ask for it. Subsequently, God grants his request, and Solomon builds an empire for himself and the nation of Israel that was the envy of all the world. He knew how life worked. Even the Queen of Sheba came for a visit from Egypt to see it (see 1 Kings 10:1).

Fast forward to the Greco-Roman world (500 BCE to 500 CE) where we find the pursuit of another source for Wisdom. These classical philosophers found what they believed to be the source of Wisdom within our transcendent design. They referred to this design using the abstract values of truth, beauty, and goodness. They believed these values (to which they referred as the three Transcendentals) perfectly harmonized with and reflected our unique intellectual, aesthetic, and moral capacities as human beings. The writings of Plato, Aristotle, and Socrates expanded these ideas and deeply influenced the development of human culture. Advances in architecture, agriculture, and the arts were seen to be the result of our transcendent human design working at its best. Modern humanism is a reincarnation of these old beliefs in the intrinsic ability of humanity to solve our own problems. Jesus came into the scene in this culture to warn about the limitations of this wisdom and redirect humanity towards a greater story, but more about this later.

Something went wrong

Both sources of Wisdom produced great results—both Solomon and the philosophies of the Renaissance. Seeking Wisdom from a Divine Being or seeking Wisdom from within our transcendent design both seemed to be effective—at least for a time. Tragically, both stories end badly. In the end, Solomon used Wisdom to control others, to fill his harem, his coffers, and his stables. Instead of using Wisdom as a guide to experience the best of being human, he exploited Wisdom as a resource for himself, and as a result everything he accomplished fell to ruins.

The age of the classical philosophers ends about the same as it did for Solomon. Despite the utopian philosophies, social order remained entrenched in the corrupt pursuit of power and pleasure, resulting in the fall of the Roman empire and the beginning of the dark ages (see Chapter 1). Just like Solomon, the Greco-Roman culture also used Wisdom as a resource. They exploited Wisdom to build society rather than use it as a guide for development of humanity, and the result was political corruption and ruin. We were so close to the answer, yet so far.

There is a pattern here. Pursue Wisdom. Accomplish great things. Exploit Wisdom for personal gain, social power, and resources. Crash and burn. It seems humanity has a long history of

THE IMPORTANCE OF BEING HUMAN

seeking Wisdom but a real problem with following it. Judging by the outcome, it seems like Solomon and the classical philosophers both got it wrong.

Well . . . yes and no. Judging by the results, they got it wrong—but there is no denying the incredible achievements of both cultures. I believe the problem was that they both had only a part of the answer. Solomon did not deal adequately with his human nature—and the result was catastrophic moral failure. The classical philosophers did not deal adequately with our divine nature—and the result was catastrophic political failure.

I believe these failures illustrate that for Wisdom to have its full benefit, we must grasp both the divine and human story in which it is based. Solomon used Wisdom to design and establish an incredible Kingdom—He believed Wisdom was Divine in origin but failed to see that it required the moral character of man for proper application. The classical philosophers used wisdom to develop an advanced society—they believed wisdom was human in origin but failed to see the necessity of moral grounding in the character and nature of the Creator.

These stories tell us that God works within the limits of His nature and character to be the source of Wisdom. But man must work within the limits of his own nature and character (what I call our divine design) to apply Wisdom. That, dear reader, is how Wisdom works.

Wisdom is a divine/human partnership

Solomon and the classical philosophers were on the right track, but they failed to see the whole picture. I believe that today not only do we fail to see the whole picture—but we have also lost sight of the whole plot! In most of the developed world today, knowledge and technology are the means and measure of progress, not Wisdom. For much of our world, Wisdom seems impractical, unmeasurable, and irrelevant. Wisdom tends to be an anachronism left to the mystics, the old, and the religious. We know we need something to help us out of the mess we are in but usually overlook Wisdom in favor of science. We need a fresh look at Wisdom for our day.

We need only look back at the life of Jesus to see a third model for Wisdom—a model entirely different from that of Solomon or the classical philosophers. Jesus lived during the same period as the classical philosophers but had a completely unique approach to life that transcended the Jewish religious culture and the Greco-Roman culture of the day. In fact, the early followers of Jesus claimed they had discovered and indeed come to know the very source of Wisdom. These early followers saw Wisdom personified in Jesus.

This inspired a whole new approach to Wisdom. These followers saw in Jesus a partnership between God and Man. This partnership based in Wisdom became the imperative of a movement that changed the world. Jesus' claim that He was "greater than Solomon" (see Luke 11:29–31) was an affront to the Jewish as well as Greek philosophies of the time. It was this Wisdom that simple fishermen would proclaim to the world (1 Corinthians 2:6–7). It was the same Wisdom as Solomon and the Greek philosophers espoused—but with a new approach. This time, it was offered in a relationship between God and man—a partnership between the created and the Creator. This was something neither Solomon nor all the Wisdom of the Greek philosophers came close to matching.

How can we follow this model for Wisdom now? Jesus' advice to His followers during His lifetime challenges us today as well: "Ask and it will be given, seek and you will find, knock and the door will be opened" (Matthew 7:7). What do we receive when we ask? Or find when we seek? Or discover when we knock? Allow me to share with you my surprising discovery. I believe Wisdom is hidden in plain sight in our divine design!

Wisdom is expressed in our divine design

The Bible is sometimes seen as a sort of "operator's manual." I have been a student of the Bible for over fifty years and personally believe it authoritatively speaks truth through human authors from God himself. But I have to ask, what exactly does the Bible as we know it today have to say about Wisdom? No doubt there are whole sections of the Bible that address the issue, but what is the real story?

Let me answer that by saying I have also been a student of Wisdom. As a student of Wisdom, I have to ask you—if the Bible is the source of Wisdom, why does it present Wisdom as something we must ask for, not study to attain (James 1:5)? Why does the Bible claim Wisdom is based on fearing God—seeing ourselves rightly in the created order of things (Proverbs 1:1–7), and not based on intelligence? And why do the followers of Jesus claim Wisdom is personified in Him, not just taught by Him (1 Corinthians 1:18–31)?

I am offering you here what I have learned from decades of asking for Wisdom, seeking it in the challenges of daily life, and knocking on doors by asking questions—lots of questions—as I try to integrate my relationship with Jesus, the source of Wisdom, and my study of the Bible into daily life. The results are far from perfect. But I am sharing what I have learned, observed, and heard from others who have done the same.

I am confident I can offer you a clear description of Wisdom because I see it expressed in our divine design. Knowing the Bible has been an invaluable tool to point me in the right direction and connect me with the divine narrative about Wisdom. But in the end, "Wisdom is revealed by her deeds" as Jesus once said (see Matthew 11:19). Wisdom is discovered by observation, not study.

So here is what I have learned from my observations, my experiences, and my faith. I believe we have three key operational components that make us a living human soul: our body, our mind, and our spirit. These operational components work together as a unit to carry out our four primary functions as human beings:

1. To live freely as individuals.
2. To live responsibly as members of a community.
3. To interact meaningfully with our world.
4. To engage positively for a future we cannot see.

Take a minute to read and reflect on these again. Incredible, isn't it?! I bet you can't help but be a bit excited—and maybe a bit intrigued—about being designed for all this, regardless of your appearance or heritage, abilities or disabilities. This is you! I am

THE IMPORTANCE OF BEING HUMAN

suggesting that the Wisdom you need to function as a human being is discoverable in your divine design—not in a book, not in a scientific study, not in any AI data pool. Wisdom is just waiting to be discovered by experiencing the design built into us by our Designer.

We all share the same operational design as human beings, regardless of how different we all look. And if we get a handle on this design and the function it serves, we can make a dramatic change in our direction as individuals and as a human family. The Wisdom woven into the fabric of our divine design is far better than knowledge or technology to guide human development. It's even better than just having a knowledge of the Bible or any other religious book—and as someone who has studied this most of his life, that is a huge statement!

You may be asking yourself, "If this is true, how is this actually useful to me in any way, shape, or form?" The idea of using our design to explore Wisdom may seem pretty far out there. But it's not as far off as it sounds. Let me explain.

It's a bit like driving a car

Let me give you a crash course in discovering the Wisdom embedded within our design. It's really not as complicated or mystical as it may seem. We do not need to depend on self-help gurus to help us find what is right in front of us—literally staring at us in the mirror! We do not need to spend hours reciting mantras or practicing new methods of self-discovery. We don't need to gather data, take a class, or become techno nerds to start using Wisdom.

It's way simpler than that. Remember, Wisdom is learned by examination of who we are. Wisdom is the skill we learn from humble, honest observation of our nature and character as human beings.

I think it's a bit like driving a car. You don't need to understand the inner workings of a car to enjoy driving it! You observe its basic operational design—how the brakes, the accelerator, and the steering wheel work—you get in the car (with a friendly instructor, of course), and you try it. You figure out pretty quickly that you need to provide fuel, maintenance, and direction, but the car does the rest. You learn how the car works operationally when you drive it. Wisdom works the same way. Once you observe the components of your basic operational design (body, mind, and spirit), you quickly learn what it is capable of doing (securing our individuality, creating love and meaning, and amplifying hope) by driving it.

The parameters of the car's design set the limits on what the car can do, just like Wisdom sets the limits on what your design can do. You become a good driver by driving within the parameters of the car's design. You become wise by living within the parameters of your divine design and letting it take you where you are designed to go.

The call of Wisdom

Our body, mind, and spirit are designed to operate together to take us down the road as individuals living in a human family. When we learn to employ these operational components properly, we discover how to live. But these roads are unfamiliar, and the journey is always a little bumpy at the start. I can tell you it becomes more enjoyable as you operate your divine design over a lifetime.

Wisdom beckons us to explore our design and its primary functions—to try taking some new roads. There is something within us that tells us we are capable of great things. It calls out to us in our homes and in our offices. Wisdom summons us to what greatness really is. It reminds us that the measure of success as a human family is not what we have achieved but how we have lived. Once you start driving with Wisdom, belief in the promises of the Enlightenment is gradually replaced by confidence in your divine design.

The groundwork for our study is complete. We are now ready to expose the myths that have held us captive to the old Enlightenment mode of operation. The promise that knowledge and technology can provide a path to greatness as a human family has failed us. It's time to reveal what Wisdom tells us about our divine design. If we let Wisdom be our guide, it will remind us of the importance of being human.

Glenn Strauss, M.D.

Chapter 4

The myth of individualism

Individualism is not all it's cracked up to be. Now just wait a minute, you say. You cannot seriously be questioning the very core of our social system, can you? Let me assure you, I have no problem with individuality or democracy. But allow me to explain the problem I have with "individualism."

The concept of "individualism" as a way of ordering society found its most profound expression in the American dream. The great experiment of American democracy was a promising start to a philosophy of natural and "inalienable," individual rights rooted in the Enlightenment. In fact, you may be surprised to hear that America in the late 1700s was the first nation founded on Enlightenment principles.

In the early 1800s, Alexis de Tocqueville famously described American individualism as a kind of "moderate selfishness," which isolated citizens from each other, putting us at risk for the "tyranny of the majority" (*Democracy in America*, 1835). I agree. Individualism is about survival, not about freedom, and this is where my problem with Individualism as a philosophy for ordering society begins. Tocqueville pointed out that "democracy" would come at the expense of slaves and native Americans. This of course eventually came true in the tragic losses of the Civil War (1860–1865).

But it didn't end there. Encouraged by the "rugged individualism" of Herbert Hoover (1928), democracy gradually became a sort of social Darwinism with the implicit goal of survival of the fittest. Theoretically, we all had an equal chance to thrive. We believed any one of us could pull ourselves up by our bootstraps to become prosperous. But the problem was, we could only do so at someone else's expense. Using this strategy, we believed we could all prosper; and prosper we did—at least some of us did.

Stripped down to its bare essentials, individualism is a strategy for ordering society built on flawed ideals. Do we really have the right to walk our own path without interference from others? Can relationships and resources be legitimately exploited because my needs are the priority? Am I truly at my best when I am on my own? I feel uneasy even asking these questions. But we must face up to the fact that we cannot have what we want without making the choices that raise these questions.

Individualism became the foundation for the claim of American exceptionalism which, by the way, does not sit well with the rest of the world. Many of my international colleagues admire the American dream and the wealth of our society but rankle at the attitude they see in us. I have no problem with democracy—I believe it to be the best system of governance. I have no problem with individuality—I believe it is the foundation for creativity and love. The problem I have with individualism is the bad idea on which it is based. The whole premise of individualism needs to be exposed as a myth.

Just imagine if everyone on the planet acted out the dream of individualism. We would live in a world of utter chaos. Inevitably, some would prosper far more than others. We love to say things like, "I've got to be me!" or, "You just do you!" But what does this even mean? How can individual actors ever be free of the other actors around them? How can we ever choose all the conditions that we need to just "be me"? Why would we even want to?

Free to be me

Let me say it another way. Using our individuality alone as the foundation for building social order (individualism) is a fatally flawed concept. Individuality I would say is good. Individualism—very bad. The idea of "free to be me" plays well in the news, on placards, from pulpits, and in political races, but it does little to address our modern social problems. In fact, I would say it has propelled us deeper into the problems!

It's strange how we work so hard to support individualism in society. It's a bit like watching a mother trying to help her children master the early childhood development concept of parallel play. The two-year-olds can survive for a while in the playpen together. But eventually they steal each other's toys and end up crying. Grownups at work and at home, surviving like two-year-olds together in the playpen, just do not paint a pretty picture! The dream of individualism is freedom, but the reality is, individualism was always about survival.

Glenn Strauss, M.D.

How bad can a little narcissism be?

Unfortunately, the problem doesn't stop with the sad picture of parallel play. Health professionals, counselors, life coaches, pastors, and teachers are overwhelmed by the increasing problem of narcissism in our society. I believe it's directly related to the promotion of Individualism. The bad ideas underlying individualism have resulted in an epidemic of restlessness, anxiety, despair, and loss of hope. I'm not trying to be cynical; I'm trying to be honest and clear. Once you believe you have the right to be whatever you want, you accept as your default position that the world revolves around you. This produces a distorted, toxic individuality—not freedom. You are, by your own choice, limited to what you can think of yourself and what you can get away with.

It's not this way with healthy individuality. We share a basic operational design with every other human being. If you pretend otherwise, you deny yourself the opportunity for the genuine freedom of healthy individuality along with healthy ways to share that individuality in community. Individualism leaves you with little chance to see a grander or bigger purpose or vision. Without a reference point in the bigger story outside of yourself, you cannot help but get a little smaller.

Sorry to say it so bluntly, but the fact that we truly believe there is freedom in individualism must be confronted for what it is—a myth that has grown out of a disconnection with our divine design. And it results in a tragic inability to experience the very thing for which we are designed—healthy individuality. Wisdom calls us to so much more.

Chapter 5

How healthy individuality inspires community

Dr. Steve Arrowsmith and I served together in international medical missions for many years. In one of our many talks about how to solve the world's problems, a particularly deep sense of despair began creeping into our hearts while looking out over yet another broken city in Africa. In the moment, I felt so stupid for investing so much in the kind of work we were doing and blurted out the question for which I was sure had no answer: Why do we persist in doing this crazy work that has so little effect? We are just a drop in the bucket. He then told me the story of Mack, the sheep dog, as told to him by Elizabeth Elliot, a well-known and seasoned missionary. Steve writes about the impact of this story on his life:

> One of my personal heroes is a woman named Elizabeth Elliot, who gained reluctant fame in the 1950s when her husband was one of five men murdered in the Amazon jungle as they tried to make contact with an isolated "prehistoric" Ecuadorian tribe. This left her widowed as a young woman and a single parent to a toddler daughter. Her next life choice was to move, with

her daughter and the sister of one of the other slain men, to live in the very village from which the murderers had come. Elizabeth, therefore, frequently had to address the "why" question. And in speech and writing she is very much a no-nonsense person, cutting to the quick of the truth, whether or not the truth is a pretty thing. And her answer is the closest to what is personally true for me as I have ever heard anyone articulate.

She describes in beautiful detail the experience of spending time in a Scottish countryside and watching a sheepdog named Mack at work. At other times, Mack acted like dogs do, lying around panting, maybe looking bored, sleeping a lot, whatever. But, when Mack was herding sheep, something entirely different happened, a profound transformation took place. Mack was a sheep dog, and when he was herding sheep, every atom in that sheep dog's body was lost in the rapture of fulfilling his purpose. His focus was total, and his joy overwhelming apparent. You see, what Mack had in that moment was that he was doing THE thing, the single thing that he had been "made" to do. His universe was in total harmony because there was not a shred of disconnect between his purpose and his actions. The challenge of getting the job done was his joy. His being and his actions were in perfect alignment. In those moments, he was able to tap into an infinite reservoir of peace and contentment.

After hearing this story, I realized this was my answer: We did this crazy work because it is what we are designed to do, and in doing it, we experienced a sense of purpose and fulfillment.

Wisdom sets you free to experience individuality

Wisdom brings you face to face with the connection between your operational design and the way you live. It exposes the myth of individualism by unveiling something far better—healthy individuality. Wisdom teaches you that your operational design defines your potential and your human limitations, not your personality, talent, or aptitude. You do not need to compare yourself to anyone else because our operational designs are all the same. Rather than eliminating weaknesses and fixing flaws to look better, you begin to discover how your operational design enables you to incorporate them into a mature self-image. We all have limitations, but you can dream about the possibility of achieving more than you can ask or think because your choices are based on your operational design, not your feelings, your limitations, or your past.

My wife and I have experienced just this sort of dreaming as we pursued a life bigger than we could have ever asked for or expected as two fairly average middle-aged people—people who, by the way, really did not like to travel. Looking back, we can hardly believe all the opportunities and blessings we have received. You, too, can learn to use your individual strengths and weaknesses, your unique personality, and your quirks to aspire for more than you might dare imagine. Just like Kim and I, all this is possible because you can observe what Wisdom teaches us about our basic design as human beings.

If you are willing to look at yourself, you can see that your operational design is what defines you, not your physical, mental, emotional, or spiritual features, and not your living conditions. You will notice that your operational design is basically the same as everyone else's and that it's well-suited to effectively navigate our chaotic world. And beyond all this, you will experience moments when you are aware of the ability to conceive of and even know the Creator.

Wisdom will never excuse the choices you make that hurt others or yourself. And it doesn't reassure you that all will be well, or that life will be fair and rewarding just because you are doing your best to live well. But it does provide a framework for how to operate according to your design—just like Mack the sheepdog enjoying his work.

Learning to drive takes time

The problem is, it takes time to learn to operate your divine operational design. It's difficult enough in the best of circumstances to learn healthy individuality, but in a culture obsessed with individualism, it's like learning how to drive at an old-timey demolition derby. Almost everyone around you is on a collision course with someone else to eliminate them as a competitor. Learning how to be an individual, when surrounded by narcissists staking out their claim to be the center of attention, takes a fearless focus on Wisdom so you don't end up in the pileup with them!

While the narcissist is wasting time souping up their cars to go faster and look better, those using their divine design are tapping into a solid engine rather than using poorly fitting "aftermarket" parts that quickly fail. The narcissist expects others to fix them when they break, blames others when they don't get where they want to go as fast as they want to get there, and generally thinks the road belongs to them.

It's hard to ignore such demanding people, especially if it's family or friends. Setting boundaries can seem more like isolation than individuality. I can assure you that, in the end, Wisdom will get you safely home to where you need to be as an individual. Wisdom is the best teacher for understanding our operational design. But you still need practice learning to use it.

How to survive the learning curve

Tragically for some, the initial operational lessons are harsh and unloving—damaging instead of developing. Rather than learning how to get through failures, some children are taught to be failures for someone else's benefit, and then shown how to do this same thing to others once they grow up. These early operational lessons are embedded deeply within us—some would say locked away in a primal part of our brain just waiting for the next threat to occur. The deep emotional pain that so many experience can cause serious problems in life, as so many people are all too aware.

It's incredible to me that as we mature, we can choose to move beyond our emotional injuries, even embrace them and forgive ourselves and others. In some cases, the damage seems irreparable, but I have seen in myself and others that our divine design is usually resilient enough to pull us through the pain on our journey to mature individuality.

Our operational design is so biased towards life that we can actually recover, even thrive after going through horrendous problems in life! The learning curve is long but doable when you have confidence that your divine design is intended to weather the storms. This confidence comes from Wisdom, not from feelings associated with old memories and habits. Feelings are healthy reactions to real experiences, good and bad. But feelings are, by definition, always reactive, not proactive, and cannot provide reliable guidance for the steps needed to grow and move forward. Only Wisdom can do that.

Tragically, the rampant growth of narcissism in our culture grows out of a belief that feelings are what define us rather than any sort of operational design, divine or otherwise. This means that millions of people are choosing how to live based on how they feel rather than how they are designed. The narcissist truly believes that personal growth is limited by submission to a "design."

Wisdom releases us from a very small world and a stunted learning curve to enjoy healthy individuality. Wisdom free us to engage and explore our world and the people in it. Embracing our design enhances and secures our individuality. We can be a little more like Mack the sheepdog joyfully herding the sheep. Wisdom drives this positive cycle of growth. Narcissism produces a toxic individuality.

Healthy individuality is not an end; it's a beginning

In the context of our modern culture, which is biased towards individualism, I believe the most important thing about healthy individuality is that it's not an end in itself. Wisdom sets us free to experience individuality in nurturing communities so we can safely explore our world and the people in it. Once you're no longer struggling to survive at someone else's expense, looking for quick fixes or making superficial modifications, then you can start contributing to your community, be it family, neighbors, colleagues, or friends. You can explore the world and the people in it without comparing, judging, or defending. You find you can give without losing anything. Life becomes a little less about right and wrong and a little more about giving and receiving. Wisdom tends to multiply in communities, and with time, becomes a rich personal resource for your own life and others.

The reality is that healthy individuality and individualism work in almost opposite ways. Individuality inspires the formation of mature, nurturing communities. It allows you to receive what is given by others rather than demand what you want. It leads to enriching relationships, not demanding interactions. Individuality helps you become your best because healthy relationships make you more of an individual, not less. While it's rare to find this today—the key to it all is Wisdom.

The basis of a healthy community and a profoundly simple social order is not the freedom to be me, but the Wisdom to be **us**.

Surely you would agree this is what we need more of today. The Wisdom of our design guides us towards strength in community, enrichment in relationships, and healthy self-awareness. All these grow from a divine design you cannot find by looking in the typical self-help book. A careful look in the mirror may help more than listening to the noisy mantras of self-improvement.

But remember, individuality alone, even within a community, is dangerous. Individuality, as an end in itself, leads to toxic individualism. True individuality, when functioning properly, always leads to a healthy community.

But here we face another problem. We must not only address the myths that undermine the development of healthy individuality, but also address the myths that wreck our ability to function as individuals—and there are many!

For the purposes of this book, we will limit our discussion to considering three specific myths that directly affect our ability to function as human beings—myths about love, meaning, and hope. Each of these myths must be exposed to free us to be the human beings we are designed to be. Wisdom exposes these myths and provides the key to proper functioning of our individuality. And as we shall see, this key is once again hiding in plain sight within our operational design.

Chapter 6

The myth that love is a feeling

"Love" in our culture is a word with a very broad meaning commonly used to express our deep satisfaction. You may love your mate, love your dog, love your children, love your job, love your friends, love your home, love your food, or love your car. You've got to admit, it feels great to love and be loved—that warm feeling of happiness and giddy satisfaction that you are where you belong and accepted for who you are. In love, life seems a happy messiness; you feel like you're on top of the world, and all is well.

We use the word "love" with so many different shades of meaning. We could easily substitute words like warmth, passion, attraction, fondness, or tenderness. Of particular interest to me, love can be understood a lot like the ancient Jewish idea of "shalom"—a sense of peaceful well-being in relationships that is given as a gift from God. I am drawn to this old idea because it communicates a deeper concept of love that I think is missing in our common usage of the word.

For those of you who have grown up in the Christian culture, the word "love" usually denotes a sense of fellowship or family. It often carries a sense of fondness and grace towards others. It was Jesus who is credited with saying, "Love your enemies." Admittedly though, it's a little confusing if you think about how Christian love is often presented. On one hand, it's viewed as a gift of a father-like God who graciously provides for us. But on the other hand, it's often preached as an obligation we have to put others first. If love is meant to be a gift, how can it be given out of obligation? I hope to clear up this confusion in the next chapter.

Frankly, most of us don't really think that deeply about love. It's just something we experience and enjoy. But still, it is a popular topic in almost every culture. Some talk about love as a transcendent force, a natural energy between people that you cannot control, something that shapes and drives our lives towards what is "good." Some cultures romanticize it as a feeling that makes you do crazy or stupid things. Still other cultures think of love as a force that binds you to the universe. I was fascinated to discover while serving in Sierra Leone that they do not even have a word for love. In Sierra Leone, their Creole translation of the Bible reads, "For God so liked [instead of loved] the world that he gave his son."

Love is important to all of us—it is truly a cross-cultural ideal, albeit with profoundly different emphases in each tradition. Regardless of your cultural background, we likely all agree at some level with the words of the song by Hal David (1965): "What the world needs now is love, sweet love."

Let the games begin

The problem is, what the world needs and what our American

culture seems to want, are two very different things. Love, once it is distorted by the myth of individualism, is not at all about what the world really needs; it's about what we as individuals want. And our narcissistic self wants to feel loved—in fact we believe it is our right. There is a sad logic to it—I believe that the right to be "me" (individualism) gives me the right to feel loved, regardless of how much it hurts anyone else (narcissism). It is incredibly shortsighted to build one myth (love is a feeling I deserve) on another myth (I can be who I want to be). We are only making our problems as a human family worse when we approach love as a feeling we deserve.

Paradoxically, the need to feel loved makes it more and more difficult to receive love. Instead of receiving love as a gift, it becomes a transactional game. You quickly learn how to keep the feeling of love going by using others as the source—not receiving it as a gift. Let the games begin!

Need I remind you how often this does not end well? You pet the dog, and he pees on your carpet. You baby your car, and the car quits or gets wrecked by some lunatic driver. You do what seems to you to be a loving gesture, and your mate says something hurtful. You do something nice for a friend, and they betray your trust. You say, "I love you," and your mate doesn't know what to say. You express your "love" for God in your prayers, and He doesn't seem to love you back by giving you what you asked for. No wonder love seems like a risky business.

Sadly, the game does not stop here! Maybe you have learned that you simply cannot depend on others to meet this need; you can only depend on yourself. So, you practice ways of feeding the need using self-love formulas and affirmation. You take "me" days, treat yourself to spas or special desserts, or do whatever you need to keep the feeling of love going. There's nothing wrong with treating yourself to good things. But if you've tried it, you know the feeling of being loved is nearly impossible to sustain from within yourself. Inevitably, you find yourself feeling unloved again.

Tragically, these cycles occur even when others love you deeply. So many friendships and marriages suffer when the partners do not see this transactional game. Husbands and wives, family and friends, often fail to provide ways for others to express their love in their own way and in their own time. Instead of being open to receiving a gift freely given, the demand to feel loved results in all sorts of self-defeating words and actions.

Let me repeat myself here: There is nothing wrong with taking care of yourself. I am only saying that the best way to take care of yourself is by receiving love, not demanding it. Receiving love is critical. Playing games to produce the feeling of love is damaging to yourself and others. I agree that you must refill your emotional gas tank, stay physically healthy, and find spiritual enrichment. Genuine love does all this. But the games we play to feed the craving to feel loved will likely lead to cycles of disappointment and, paradoxically, to the pain of feeling not just unloved but unlovable. The myth that love is a feeling I deserve has grave consequences. It's scary what we are willing to do to feel loved. It's even worse what happens when we give up on the possibility.

What's love got to do with it?

The fact that being loved does produce feelings is not the problem. These feelings are a wonderful gift! The problems emerge when you obsessively feed the need to feel loved. With years of counseling experience behind me, I have seen again and again how often people lack the skills and awareness needed to receive love. Many have spent years and thousands of dollars trying to sustain the feeling of being loved, never realizing it has been offered freely by those around them.

Let me save you a lot of time and money by laying it out plainly. Here's what happens when you focus on feeding the need to feel love: First, you start believing you are the only one who can make yourself feel truly loved. Soon, the time and energy you spend to love others begins to compete with your ability to love yourself. So, guess what? You start to use others to fill your tank and then rationalize the exploitation as something that you deserve.

These are all really bad ideas for good mental health. Gradually worn down by unmet expectations for feeling loved, we start sliding down a slippery slope of increasing manipulation of others. Deep down, you realize the hypocrisy and craziness of it, but gradually the manipulation you use to feel loved seems to be completely justified. It may sound strange or politically incorrect today, but believing we have the right to feel loved leads to dark places within ourselves and the exploitation of others. The myths about love are at the core of many of our problems today. I can see why many people question the possibility of having a truly loving relationship. What's love got to do with it, you ask? Good question!

I think you would agree this is not what any of us want. Yet we persist in trusting self-defeating strategies built around the expectation that I can and must feel loved—all the time. It may be scary to admit, but genuine love has nothing to do with the feeling you hope to keep feeding. I say again that the feeling is good, but it's not the point.

Who cares as long as it feels good

I see this transactional approach to love play out day after day all around me. After all, love is big business. The myth about love permeates everything from entertainment to science. It's the dream played out in movies and in romantic novels. It's built into the algorithms of dating apps designed to help us find the right person, at the right time, in the right place, with the right chemistry to produce the right feeling. There is nothing wrong with dating apps per se, but I believe they feed our distorted belief that love is a chemistry problem. Think about it: How can we love everyone if all we expect is to love the one person who fits our dating app profile?

Why do we perpetuate this insanity? We sincerely believe that if it feels good and it doesn't seem to hurt anyone, then do it! Who cares as long as it feels good, right? My point is that with this kind of thinking, we fall into all sorts of craziness. We lose so much more than we gain. Make no mistake: We do need to be loved, and we are designed to give and receive it. But we so easily substitute our healthy and instinctual need to express and experience love with our need to feel loved. We are too willing to trust that good feelings meet our legitimate needs.

Fortunately, Wisdom gives us a much better idea of how we

are designed to express and experience love. If we pay attention to this design as we will discuss in the next chapter, I believe we can address much of the chaos in our own lives and in our society.

Glenn Strauss, M.D.

Chapter 7

How boundless love is created

What if I told you that you are a love making machine? Ok, don't get too excited. I know the idea sounds weird, but I'm trying to emphasize that we are designed (body, mind, and spirit) to create love, not just feel it. Consider a couple of examples. There's nothing like the love of a small child. I wish I had savored it more when my children were young. Over the years, our four kids and five grandchildren all displayed an abundance of it towards my wife and me, and we towards them. Love was not about producing a feeling—there was no transactional game at play. Just nestled down in our lap, reading a book together, sharing dinner at the table, enjoying a game, or doing a chore together—love was created in those activities.

My wife and I have shared such moments together thousands of times over the last 50 years. What is perhaps a little strange is how love is created. It happens when we are doing something together, but the activity doesn't really seem to matter. Or when we are sharing a dream or idea, but it's not about the dream. Or when we are laughing, but it's not about the joke. When I try to sing a romantic song—but we both end up crying. I've learned that love happens between two people when body, mind, and spirit are open and fully engaged in life together. Something is created that is more than a feeling, more than a memory, more than an activity. It can't be fully captured in a picture or with words. No other being is capable of such an experience because no other being is designed to create love. I only wish I were better at it!

Maybe this is why something as simple as sharing a meal together can be so powerful. I have a fond memory of a time when a wise friend was preparing a gourmet meal for us. He pointed out that preparing a meal and sharing it together is really an expression of love. It is so true! All the senses were engaged as we talked while the meal was being prepared, smelled the savory aromas, enjoyed the beautiful presentation, and then sat and enjoyed it together. The conversation was deep and meaningful. We experienced life as something bigger than us—we shared together in a gift. It was a great meal in more ways than one! This story has been repeated many times over at our dinner table creating wonderful memories with children and grandchildren, friends and neighbors.

What can I say? It's a gift

Healthy love is a gift. But it's not a gift added to life like some bonus deal . The gift is built into us! Our operational design can create love! The same design that we experience as we develop healthy individuality also gives us the power to create unlimited love. Wisdom calls us to use our divine design to create loving experiences.

Let me say it another way. Love is not something we have or

don't have for others. It's not some magical feeling we possess or give away. Nor is it an expression of warmth that certain personalities have and others do not. Love is something created by using our divine design as we experience the journey of life together with Wisdom as our guide.

Think about the implications of that for a minute. Love is not some kind of emotional resource I have to manage. I do not have to choose how much emotional energy to spend on myself or others. It's not a zero-sum game where there are winners and losers. I do not have to choose between loving myself and loving others. Incredibly, we have all been given a design that, when operated wisely, creates love for ourselves and others. This kind of love is boundless because it's generated by our design. This means as long as we are alive, whether we are rich or poor, sick or healthy, we can continue to love.

Sounds like a lot of work

You may be thinking that love is starting to sound like a lot of work! If Wisdom calls us to create love, not just feel it, we might have to start doing something, and not just wait for it to happen to us. You are correct. But start doing what exactly? If our divine design is a gift that generates love, how do we get the generator running? Is love produced automatically just because I got out of bed today? Obviously not.

It turns out, love is generated when our operational design reflects the image of its Creator. Love is the creative means to express the love of the One who created us. Love is not a feeling.

Love is not a resource. Love is the intentional and fundamental expression of the Creator of our operational design, a design given as a gift to human beings.

To really wrap your head around this, you will need to set aside for a minute any preconceived religious notion of a Supreme Being and consider a Creator who is revealed by and in us! This is what the Bible actually means when it says we are created in the image of God. It means our Creator is willing to endow us with the same ability to love that He himself possesses. I am not saying the Creator made us some sort of deity—that much seems clear. But I am also saying that we are not cheap knockoffs either. Our divine qualities are the real deal expressed in flesh and blood. Love is the epitome of the divine characteristics that we have been designed to display in our human nature.

Wisdom calls us to display this divine design, as only human beings can, by putting love out on the table like a meal for others to enjoy with us. This is why I say love is both the intentional and fundamental expression of our Creator; at its core, love is fundamentally the reflection of a divine design, intentionally put on display by human beings. That's what creates love. And this is a meal worth having every day!

I thought you said it was free

But there is sort of a catch. Our design as human beings made in the image of the Creator is a gift that costs us nothing. But there is a price to pay for the journey it takes us on. There is no charge for the design—but there is a cost in using the design. There is something required of us to use our design.

Let me explain by going back to our car analogy. We already talked about how discovering our design is a bit like learning to drive a car. It's important to realize that when you get into the car to drive it, you do so while trusting that the car will work correctly. You trust the design of your car to do what it's supposed to do—trusting that brakes will always stop you when needed. You trust that the designers did a good job of making it safe! That's the kind of trust I'm talking about here—trusting that our Designer did a good job and that our design will do what it's supposed to do every single time we employ it. To drive a car, you must trust in its design. It's the same with our design as human beings.

But there is another cost that comes with using a car. You don't get anywhere for free. It's not enough to just trust that the car works; you must also figure in the cost of fuel, maintenance, licensing, and insurance. It's the same with using our divine design as human beings. There is a cost to driving our "car"—a cost for using our design to create love. For us as human beings, the cost is the price of our ego. The reason for this is simple: Love is created to be given away, and ego wants to keep what you have. Love requires giving away a bit of yourself.

Let me use the example of my own life to explain this one. I have performed professionally as a musician, a public speaker, and as a surgeon literally thousands of times over many years for thousands of people. The enormous resources I have spent to master these things is a cost fully loaded into each and every event, surgery, and performance. It's the cost I have freely paid to provide others, as best I can, with good eyesight, encouragement, or musical enrichment. In the process, I give something of myself away that cannot be recovered in a paycheck or a donation or applause.

So, what keeps me going? It's not the paycheck! The fact is, you cannot pay me enough to consistently do my very best. All you can do is trust that what I offer is my best. I, not you, must pay the price in terms of practice, priority, and perseverance to use my best to meet your needs. Thankfully, donations and paychecks support and encourage the effort, but it's not what makes me willing to use my best for your benefit. I must pay the price to give my best, and this is the very definition of love. To choose otherwise puts my interests, my ego, at the center. This is why I say that ego is the price we pay to create love.

In my mind, there is no greater example of this than a healthy marriage. Marriage can be a truly beautiful display of divine design at work. Amazing love is generated by two individuals working together with weaknesses and limitations exposed but sharing equally as human beings in a divine design. It requires trust that our design is good, and it costs us our egos to embrace a true partnership with someone else. But it magnificently displays the love of the One who created both man and woman. It's why sex without love is pleasurable but not fulfilling. It's why saying "I love you" without love is charming but empty. Why sharing dreams without love is fun but fanciful. In marriage we use our bodies to act in love. We use our minds to speak in love. We use our spirits to connect in love as man and woman.

Let me be clear here: It costs something to create and give away what you have created. But when I stop seeing love as a resource and instead trust that it's an act of creation for which I am designed, I begin to experience the cost of lovingly giving my best in a different way. I can confidently use my skills and aptitudes to create love and trust that my design won't fail. It's stunning once you see this truth! We can create without using up any resources. Love is not self-destructive. Quite the opposite. When love is created out of our design, we are never used up. We are expanded and strengthened!

This is what makes love boundless and free, not an obligation. It's why, at our best, we are sacrificial and fearless in our love of others. It's the reason I could do my best every day to perform thousands of eye operations for free in the mission field for many years. It's why I can volunteer my time to help others grow. It's the reason we can give our best to our children or our spouse year after year expecting nothing in return.

We are all designed to fearlessly express and experience love like we hear in the story of Mack the sheepdog working in the field, a small child sitting in our lap, a loving spouse sharing something we can never repay, a musician giving a performance, or a surgeon giving their best. We are designed to create love and give it away, even in the imperfect ways we often do. Wisdom stirs us to create, give, and receive love.

Once again, the contrast between healthy love and love as a feeling is striking. I am able to create love by engaging my divine design, not just feel love. I can love sacrificially, putting aside my ego, because love is not a zero-sum game. Love of others never competes with love of self. The myth of love as only a feeling leads to weakness and exploitation. The Wisdom that creates love leads to fearless and boundless love for self and others.

Glenn Strauss, M.D.

Are we there yet?

We are not quite to the end of our story of our human design yet. I hope this book has rattled your cage enough to provoke some serious thought. But we are not quite to the end of our discussion about what it means to be human. So far, we have seen that individuality properly developed and operating under the influence of Wisdom produces divine love. Individualism and the need to feel love are exposed by Wisdom as dehumanizing myths that produce social chaos.

But here is where we face another major challenge—it's not enough to know our potential without knowing how to get there. This is where I must challenge your thinking again. We could end our discussion right here except for the fact that we don't realize that the components of our divine design (body, mind, and spirit) are meant to function seamlessly together as a unit with a clear purpose. How did we lose sight of this critical concept?

In the next two chapters we will expose the emptiness and the tragic social consequences of the compartmentalized life we have naively accepted as normal. Our culture has produced a problem of existential proportions for us as a human family. Our compartmentalized life has reduced us to being shallow commodities, leaving us blind to the meaning and significance found in the purpose of our design.

We must discover how Wisdom restores the ability to navigate the enormous complexity of our world as human beings and how this ability restores meaning and significance to our lives. We must expose the real cost of living in a fragmented society—and hope it's not too late to pull ourselves back together!

Glenn Strauss, M.D.

Chapter 8

The myth of finding meaning in our busy, compartmentalized lives

Our Western culture is a complex web of silos all vying for our attention. For starters, we have the family silo, the work silo, and the church silo. We are careful to avoid bringing work home with us or to bring home to work. On the spiritual side, religion is generally confined to experiences in our church, mosque, or synagogue. We manage a spiritual life, a home life, and a work life, all with surprisingly little overlap. We wear many different hats.

Add to these silos the "me" space we create for ourselves. We go to the gym to work on our body, do self-help courses to improve our mind, or take in a concert or an art museum to expand ourselves. Our lives are highly compartmentalized. We try our best to be successful in each of life's silos, keenly aware that each silo has its own definition of success, and often gravitating to the silo in which we have the most success and feel the safest.

Why do we choose to live with this compartmentalized complexity? Is it because we find this way of doing life particularly meaningful or satisfying? The real reason is sadly apparent if you are willing to look: It's all about the payoff!

Glenn Strauss, M.D.

Think for a minute about how we reward success in our American culture. Each silo has its own way of rewarding success. Career success is rewarded with position and finances; success at home with happiness and peace; success at church with belonging and recognition. Our compartmentalized life hands out its rewards from within each silo. Paradoxically, our culture also rewards those who break out of these cultural silos. The extraordinary athletes, the smartest tech developers, the politician who gets something done, the preacher who brings in the crowds, the brilliant musician or artist, all get a pass on normal cultural silos. These seemingly lucky few have discovered how to capitalize on a highly compartmentalized personal life built on some extraordinary physical, mental, or creative aptitude. Who cares if their life as a whole is a mess. We see them as heroes of nonconformity.

Once someone points it out, it's hard to miss the fact that our system of rewards drives us towards the social and personal compartmentalization that our culture values. There is little reward for being an all-around good guy. Sorry about pointing this out—it's a real bummer for all you nice folks out there. There is no tangible reward for being a great human being or living a full life. Our culture does not reward a life well-lived, except maybe for a few exaggerated words at a funeral. And it doesn't do us much good then! Balance or holism are things we pursue only when we are falling apart trying to succeed. We take a yoga class or medicate ourselves and then move on the best we can with our complex lives. This only perpetuates the myth that our only hope for finding meaning or significance in life is in our silos, embracing what life has to give us: possessions and recognition for achievement.

It's just business

Maybe I shouldn't take it so seriously. After all, this is just the way things work. From childhood to retirement, we are "rewarded" to work in our silos—we get that pat on the back from a parent, a specific achievement, or that bonus for a certain job well done. We naively expect that if we stick to the cultural script, there will be credit where credit is due. But then we discover that life is not fair! We are told, often condescendingly and with just enough empathy to make it believable, that it's just business; it's not personal. But the reality is, it's very personal.

Every one of us has felt the frustration of being unappreciated and undervalued when we go unrewarded for our best efforts at work or at home. No matter how many times someone says you are special or that your life has value, it's tainted by the realization that no one is stepping up to give you a seat at the head of the table. We eventually grow tired of hearing the cliché statements of appreciation and reading our personnel file full of overused affirmations about our valued contributions to the success of the business. The "reward" seems to speak for itself: We are not worth as much as we think we are to others. Meaning and significance go right out the window with our much sought-after rewards.

But the situation is much worse than that. Consider how we talk about the cost of war, the cost of immigrant lives, the cost of health care, the cost of climate change—the list goes on and on as endless political debate. These are lives we are talking about here, not costs. I certainly understand there are economic considerations for doing life, but this preoccupation with cost of life goes beyond economic considerations to what has become an economic definition of human life.

Are you aware, for example, that the airline industry has a formula for how much each passenger's life is worth so they can calculate return on investments for safety improvements and maintenance? It's true. Last I heard, you are worth about $250K. Seems a little low to me.

Advertisers know how much your particular demographic is worth to them. Actuaries calculate the cost of life to keep insurance companies profitable. It's disturbing to think someone has calculated my cost to society and then asked me to pay for it. It's a bit too much like the dystopian story portrayed in the 1976 film, *Logan's Run*, in which equilibrium between resources and population is maintained by killing everyone over 30.

My point is this: When money is used to calculate our value, when life becomes a business, the picture of humanity gets completely distorted and the meaning for life is lost. When we go down the path of placing monetary value on human life, in the end, we all end up being a commodity instead of feeling valued or having meaning. And once human life is measured as a commodity defined and valued by its silo, disastrous social injustice becomes the norm. We become the consumed, not just the consumer.

I am worth it

The messages of modern consumerism amplify the myth that we can find meaning and significance in our achievements and possessions. The needs created by individualism are easy to exploit.

THE IMPORTANCE OF BEING HUMAN

Businesses love it when you say, "I'm worth it." Every marketing expert knows how stupid we become when we see shiny new things glittering before us. We happily comply with advertisements by purchasing what we don't really need so we can have what we don't really want.

I think it's fair to say that If narcissism is the child of individualism (Chapter 4), consumerism is its significant other! It's a little shocking to think of all the ways we're exploited by businesses and how tolerant we are of what it has done to us. Yet, we consistently opt for more stuff and less value—more achievement and less meaning. "Self" has become the biggest silo of all!

Never before in history has so much stuff meant so little to so many. What we have is largely taken for granted. It's all about what we don't have but believe we so richly deserve. Our cultural expectation of reward has created an unpayable debt of entitlement. As firm believers in individualism, we want to do what we want to do, have what we want to have, go where we want to go. a we ndwant to be rewarded for it; in fact, we believe wholeheartedly that we are entitled to it!

Convinced that we must count for something, and often frustrated by lack of reward from others, we create rewards for ourselves, various "payments" that help us feel valued. We truly believe we "owe it to ourselves" to have that bigger car, nicer house, or better pay. Some are willing to work for these rewards; others just consider it a right. Some are even willing to steal for it! Together, narcissism and consumerism drive our fragmented lives to the edge of meaninglessness. The result is often a life of unfulfilled expectations, a nagging sense of entitlement, and gradual compromise of social values to get what we feel we deserve.

God helps those who help themselves, right?

It doesn't help to give God the credit for our mess! Algernon Sidney is credited with the now famous saying, "God helps those who help themselves" (*Discourses Concerning Government*, 1698). It upsets me when I hear people quote this as a Bible verse. It was really a snide remark about the powerlessness of God and the proper role of government to empower us as individuals. Sorry if I'm bursting your bubble, but God does not sprinkle a little meaning on your achievements and possessions like fairy dust. And it's most certainly not the role of government to empower us!

Sidney's statement helped convince the Christian majority in early America that God's plan was being protected by a government that encouraged individual initiative. "God helps those who help themselves" quickly became the doctrinal statement of American exceptionalism—we had God on our side. Who could possibly be more significant than we Americans?

My wife and I were often embarrassed in our travels by the perception of American arrogance and entitlement. We saw the patronizing attitudes in American missionaries, visiting pastors, doctors, politicians, and even American crews on international flights. I am sorry to say we even saw it in ourselves. Fortunately, we learned early on that we are not so special. Not that there is anything wrong with the American dream for prosperity, health, and happiness. But when the dream became our birthright, certified by God Himself, we let pride get the better of us.

Tragically, "one nation, under God" as it says in our Pledge of Allegiance, has gradually become more about living under the banner of God's presumed approval of everything we want rather than living under God's authority. The feeling of American exceptionalism is dying at the hand of our own pride. That's probably a good thing. The problem is that much of our sense of personal significance is dying with it.

It all just makes me tired

The myth that meaning and significance are found in our achievements and possessions ultimately wears us out. There is simply no way to sustain a life in which I reward myself for everything I do, get everything I deserve, and become everything I want. J.D. Rockefeller was once asked: "How much money is enough?" He famously replied, "Just a little bit more." We can only be disappointed by the secret dream of having it all.

But we try anyway, restlessly clinging to the dream, following the path of least resistance to the greatest reward in our fragmented culture. No wonder "burnout" is so common. Our operational components are not designed for this kind of stress. Though we may tell ourselves over and over again that everyone matters, and that "things" cannot make us happy, judging by our behavior, we clearly do not believe it. I believe we are paying the price for it.

Wisdom exposes the fallacy of trying to extract meaning from our possessions and achievements. The good news is that Wisdom shows us a better path to meaning and significance. In our next chapter, we will consider how to use our human operating system to create meaning and significance rather than be consumed by our cultural myth of finding meaning in our compartmentalized lives.

Chapter 9

How our divine design creates meaning and significance

Our Creator has given us an incredible tool with which to work: our divine design. In fact, it's a tool made in the actual image of the Creator. It's the strength of our divine design that enables us to navigate the complex world and the challenges it brings. This is not American exceptionalism; it's human exceptionalism!

For reasons we cannot understand, it turns out that our body, mind, and spirit can make life in this world work. No one part of our design will do, despite what our compartmentalized culture rewards. We were designed by the Creator of all things as a complete operating unit to be just what this world needs. I hope those of you who may question the validity of this statement will give me a chance to explain.

Trying for the hat trick

It's tempting to think of the three components (body, mind, and spirit) that run our human design as three separate components. In our compartmentalized cultural context, we might think that evolution pulled off some kind of hat trick, leading to the formation of a superior being. (For those of you a bit lacking in knowledge of sports lingo like me, the "hat trick" refers to a single hockey player scoring three goals in one game.) Evolution proposes that an adaptable, mechanically flexible body got together with the world's biggest brain and a creative spirit in one animal to make it superior to all the other animals. There are some truly elegant theories about how all this could have happened, but I must say it lacks a certain believability. There is just not enough evidence for these stories to really be convincing unless it is just what I want to believe.

It is especially popular in our modern culture to think of the spirit as separate from our mind and body. This concept is called "dualism." It's a convenient belief for those who want to deal with life as a science experiment explained by provable facts and leave the subjective stuff for others to deal with. It is also quite useful for those who prefer to keep their religion out of their personal life. But more about all this in a bit.

Back to the evolutionary hat trick. Are we a collection of mutations or instead, a well-designed operating unit? Wisdom says we were formed as one single operating unit—body, mind, AND spirit. Our operational parts did not show up randomly, finally getting together over millions of years. My point is that if body, mind, and spirit were formed as a unit, then it only makes sense that we function best when they are used as a unit. I would propose that we experience what it means to be fully human when we are component parts are fully integrated.

There is another kind of "hat trick" that I have used since I became a follower of Jesus over fifty years ago. It involves a trick

I employed to try as best I could to integrate the three components of my design: body, mind, and spirit. The "trick" was to do life wearing only one hat—pretty simple. It was one of the best choices I ever made, next to marrying my sweet wife. I could have worn many hats but chose to wear only one as best I could. I did not wear a doctor hat, a dad hat, a teacher hat, a home and garden hat, a leisure hat, a pastor hat, a missionary hat, and a musician hat. I did all these things, but I learned how to do them wearing one hat.

I don't remember ever being a "Sunday Christian" except before I was a Christian. Once I invited the Creator to use me as His image bearer as an act of faith, I chose to focus on doing life as God had designed me. I believe I am made in the Creator's image, transformed and equipped by faith to live in a new world that the Creator is restoring right in the middle of the old one. This is the one hat I choose to wear as best I can. I have no idea where that idea came from—but I am thankful to this day for it.

As I have gotten older, I see much more clearly that I am actually designed as a human being to wear this one hat. Not only do I have a purpose, but I am also designed for that purpose as a human being, not as Dr. Glenn Strauss. The "one hat" trick helped me establish a healthy individuality in the context of a highly compartmentalized culture. It helped me embrace my personal limitations rather than avoid them and accept my strengths without trying to exploit them for my purposes. Most importantly, it reminded me that I am a spiritual being in a physical world. All the other "hats" offered by my culture could never do this. They are all far too small for my divine design.

I now believe I understand a bit more of how this works. So I am humbly and urgently sharing this with you because you have the same design as I do. Without realizing it, you may be trying to force too many different hats to fit your design as a human being.

Curious? I hope so. This one idea could change everything about how you live. I ask for a little patience as I try to lay this all out for you in more detail. It all comes together in our design to create meaning and significance in our own lives and the world around us.

What's so important about being human?

Chances are, you have thought to yourself more than once that life seems meaningless. You don't want to be a Gloomy Gus, yet you can't help but wonder. So, let me ask you: What if you are correct? You sense the shallowness of your busy-ness, the emptiness of the rewards you pursue, and the insignificance of the possessions you have. You are quite aware that you are replaceable. What if life itself is essentially meaningless?

Before you despair, let me ask another question that I hope will ignite your imagination: What if life is not designed to bring meaning to us—rather, we are designed to bring meaning to life? What if we are designed to create significance in our relationships and through our day-to-day tasks instead of depending on the conditions and experiences of our compartmentalized, commercialized life to make us feel valued and significant?

This book has been leading up to this point: The single most important thing about our basic human design is that it is intended to bring meaning and love to life. In a very real sense, we create both love and meaning by fully utilizing the divine design we have been given. This means that even the things that seem mundane take on importance when we wear our "human being" hat.

It's like a fusion reaction

Think of it like a nuclear fusion reaction in which energy is produced by combining atoms. We are designed as human beings so that when we combine body, mind, and spirit, a tremendous amount of energy is produced. We already discussed how our design produces love in Chapter 7. Even more important is that our divine design produces meaning and significance as a sort of "energy." I am not talking about some sort of metaphysical or mystical force. I am saying that practically speaking, our design can give meaning and substance to what we are doing or saying.

Here's how it looks: Your friendly conversation with a neighbor about their dog, your extra effort to do the dishes for your mate, your encouraging words to your child, your caring encounters with people at work, etc.—all these seemingly small things often take on meaning and significance far beyond the simple act. The friend can see they are not alone, your spouse knows they are supported and respected, your teammate experiences a sense of being valued, all from a few very simple actions. I have no doubt you, too, have experienced this in one way or another. My point is that it's a real thing. It is not some feeling we get; these are spiritual interactions between two spiritual/physical beings.

I think you can see how dualistic thinking (viewing our spiritual nature as completely separated from our physical nature) would undermine your ability to generate this fusion reaction by "disconnecting" our spirit from our body and mind. Dualism disconnects us from all things spiritual by making spirituality a mental exercise. For this reason, just like individualism hides individuality, dualism neutralizes our ability to create love and meaning.

Please note that I am not trying to give mystical significance to everyday events—in fact, just the opposite. A flat tire is just a flat tire. I am only saying that how you engage with everyday events has great significance, even mundane tasks like changing a flat tire. The key is to approach it as a human being with body, mind, and spirit "fused" together. Wouldn't it be incredible if everything in life, big or small, the good things and the bad, all had significance effortlessly generated by our "fusion engine" running on divine design?

I'm only human

But what about our human limitations? Do these limitations keep us from experiencing the "fusion reaction" of our divine design? I am not talking about our personal limitations—like how tall we are— though these are important to consider. I am talking about how the limitations of our operational design such as needing food, water, sleep, and exercise might affect our "fusion engine." Do these physical limitations keep us from achieving our potential? I would say quite the opposite is true. Our limitations are an essential part of our human design and contribute to our potential.

We disparagingly use the phrase "I'm only human" to excuse

our mistakes as if to say we cannot expect our design to work very well considering how imperfect it is. I say we should view our design as an extraordinary gift and our limitations as a blessing! We have limitations because we are human. Consider for a moment the ancient story of Man in the Garden of Eden.

When the Creator (as the story goes) put the limits on what Adam and Eve could eat in the Garden of Eden, it was for their own protection. He asked them not to eat of the "Tree" of the Knowledge of Good and Evil because its fruit was not compatible with their design. Clearly it was more than an ordinary tree. Rather than nourishing them, the Creator knew it would overload their design. Unfortunately, they bought the Disrupter's (Satan's) lie that they could exceed their design specifications with no consequences. The result was long, slow self-destruction along with a barrier erected between them and the Creator and exile from their birthplace in the Garden.

I love this story because it reminds me that contrary to popular belief, the Creator knew our limitations not only protect us: they define us. These limitations are part of our operational design. Our limitations mean we do not walk through walls, live in the ocean, or plug ourselves into a USB port to upload data or into a wall socket when we are running low on energy. We cannot go without sleep, food, or water. Like every person on earth, we suffer if we try to do what we are not designed to do, but we benefit if we operate within our design.

Glenn Strauss, M.D.

It's all good

When we fully express our divine design (limitations and all), we find that meaning and love show up around us. I do not understand how this happens. I only know by observing that when our fusion engine is running, it does! How else can you explain a simple act of love changing someone's life? Or a word of encouragement starting a lifetime of service to others? How is it possible that our impact on others and our world can be so radically out of proportion to what we say or do?

I loved telling my eye teams to watch for how small things we do for our patients can have huge effects. I can only explain this if meaning is something created. By using our divine design, we bring meaning to what we do and say. We bring meaning to our individuality, to the love we create, and to the communities we form. We do that—not fate, not rewards, not even God. He has designed us so that we bring meaning and significance into our world as those who bear His image.

The world is a chaotic mess. It's not able to restore itself to order. It's not self-correcting. It's why we were designed by the Creator for the role of Creation Administrator. But to successfully fill this role, human beings can and must live out the design we have been given. This brings goodness and peace into the messy world, just like God in the beginning brought good into the chaos and darkness. Creating love and meaning in our world is an incredible privilege and a solemn responsibility. It's what is so incredibly important about being human in our world today.

Just reflect on this for a minute before you read on. Let me summarize for your reflection: If we can avoid the compartmentalization of body, mind, and spirit, these operational components of our design create meaning and significance, love and community. Our cultural myths result in individualism, consumerism, narcissism, and dualism that lead to emptiness. Each and every one of these "isms" is extraordinarily destructive to us and to our world and leads us away from what it means to be human.

The truth is, these myths inevitably lead to dehumanization and will eventually result in total chaos in the family of humanity. On the other hand, Wisdom results in healthy individuality, boundless love, community, and meaning. Wisdom restores and reminds us of our importance as human beings to our world and enables us to produce the incredible fruit of significance and peace that our world needs.

We have one last thing to consider. We must discuss what fuels our design. What produces enough energy to create love and meaning? What triggers the fusion reaction of our operational components to produce the creative energy for which they are designed? Sometimes it feels like we are running on empty. I would say that just avoiding the myths of our culture is not enough. We must expose one final myth and discover how hope fuels the fusion reaction that energizes our lives.

Glenn Strauss, M.D.

Chapter 10

The myth of power in positive thinking

Many of us grew up reading *The Little Engine That Could,* an American folktale from the early 1900s about the power of positive thinking. I've read it to my kids dozens of times: "I think I can, I think I can, I think I can." They just loved how that sounded like a train on the tracks. We cheered for the little engine when it finally made it to the top of the hill, and then came sighing with relief all the way back down: "I thought I could, I thought I could." I truly wish it were this simple. Most of us grew up believing the promises of the Enlightenment (Chapter 2). We were confident we could reason our way to a better world. Clearly, we haven't. Or perhaps we just can't. We trusted the promises of Enlightenment only to end up with an age of skepticism, division, and isolation.

Why do we still persist in our idea that with a little positive thinking, we can still set things right for ourselves and our world? Maybe it's partly because it's easy to experience short-term benefits of positive thinking. Or maybe it's because we truly believe that since we solved the problem of mobile communication and data sharing, we can obviously solve the problem of world hunger and injustice. "Just Believe" say the T-shirts. "Stay positive" we say, and together we will be unstoppable. If there is any energy created by this positive thinking, I certainly cannot see it except in very short bursts and on a very small scale. Otherwise, it's the big mess of life as usual, and we are all too tired to do anything about it.

Maybe deep down we realize the absurdity of "brain power," but we just can't help ourselves. Be honest—am I the only one who has tried to levitate a spoon with their mind? And considering a world population that continues to replace itself every hundred years or so, the idea of transforming 8 billion lives with positive thinking alone is just plain nonsense. Even social media cannot solve this problem. Maybe this is why we cling to the idea that the best we can do is have positive thoughts in the moment. Never mind that the train is heading for a bridge that is out.

We want to believe that the world can be changed one person at a time if we just think positively. We have been schooled in the Enlightenment ideal that we can think our way to a better future. We mistake the ability to do what I need to do in the moment (produced by healthy, positive thinking) for the power to transform myself and my future. We have a fundamental misunderstanding of the process for change.

Certainly, positive thinking is helpful for achieving concrete, obtainable, personal goals in the short term—positive thinking is good and does affect the near future. Positive people have more energy, look for solutions not problems, and address crises with optimism. But it does not give them power over the long-term future. As much as we would like to believe it, positive thinking is not a tool for change—at least not by itself.

THE IMPORTANCE OF BEING HUMAN

"I need more power, Scotty!"

I am a long-time *Star Trek* fan. I particularly love those scenarios when all hope is gone, and Captain Kirk passionately appeals to Scotty, the engineer, for more power. "I'm giving her all she can take, Captain," he would say as Captain Kirk pushes the Enterprise beyond its limits to save the day once again. Many of us live life this way. We learn to "give her all she can take," using the power of positive thinking to push through each challenge. We choose to survive by living in the moment, hoping that what we do now will pave the way to a better future that is out of our control. Deep down, we have no substantial hope for the future. We often see the "future" as an extension of whatever we can secure in the present and no more.

Again, I am not arguing with the value of positive thoughts. Who doesn't get a little inspired by the teachings of Master Yoda. "Do or do not. There is no try," says the Jedi Master. He believed in using the power of the positive side of the force to balance the negative dark side of force. For a Jedi knight, all that matters to win is right in front of you. Block everything else out. Hope is irrelevant.

Some of us are very good at living in the moment. Others just seem to naturally hang out in the past or future. Like me for example. I easily get bogged down in the paralysis of analysis, labeling everything as good or bad. I can see the train wreck coming and miss what is happening right in front of me. It can be paralyzing.

I had to learn the value of living in the moment from my wife who is, let's say, "time challenged." To my great surprise, I have discovered many benefits from living positively in the moment, assuming the best until proven wrong. I'm not great at doing so, but at a personal level it just feels better to stay positive than to be negative. As a "glass half full" kind of guy, I'm more upbeat, more energized to do the tasks at hand. I can certainly accomplish more today if I'm positive about what I can rather than cannot do.

Relationships are better, too. Constantly assigning meaning based on hurtful past experiences or patterns of unmet expectations will hinder receptiveness to the love your friend or spouse has for you right now. Negativity shuts the door to relational growth.

As a side note, let me mention here an important point about how we think. We have both conscious and subconscious thoughts, and both affect us. Positive thinking is a choice for our conscious mind, not the subconscious. Interestingly, we often refer to bad behaviors as "thoughtless." That is actually correct. Most (not all) destructive behaviors originate at a subconscious level. The fact is, whatever thoughts we have at a conscious level, even very positive thoughts, unfortunately cannot stop subconscious thoughts from affecting us.

Almost everyone has experienced irrational fears or anger or embarrassment. We've been at that point when something triggers a reaction way out of proportion to the actual events. Positive thoughts do not seem to have the power to stop these reactions. In fact, the key to managing them is consciously accepting the negative thoughts, not hiding them under a pile of positivity. But that is a topic for others to address.

Am I all that I need?

This brings us to the real problem underlying the belief in the "power" of positive thinking: It is dangerously aligned with the myth of individualism (Chapters 4 and 5). Positive thinking makes complete sense in a world where I believe I am all that I need (or all I can really depend on); where as a matter of survival, there is no room for negativity, doubt, or uncertainty. Positive thoughts for a narcissist act as a sort of guard at the gate of their self-image. It's essential for their own well-being and success to maintain the belief that they must stay in control at almost any cost including broken relationships and marriages, personal burnout, and depression.

Positive thinking is indeed "powerful" in a sense. It works well for many tasks because our mental capacity is remarkable. But it takes considerable personal resources to keep these thoughts going as a defense against the feeling of powerlessness. Eventually, these resources get used up and cannot be easily replaced. The affirmations that keep us going in our belief that we have the power to control the future eventually become empty noise in a world out of our control.

There is hope

In the end, the future usually comes down to the choices, behaviors, and words of lots of people over the long term. True, we need positive thoughts in the moment to make the best choices we can. But these thoughts have no power to shape our future or erase our past. It's too complicated for that to work. We need something more powerful than positive thoughts. We need hope! Hope is what connects us as mortal beings with the future.

Wisdom exposes the myth that there is power in positive thinking and reveals how hope fuels our lives. The myth of power in positive thinking leads to disillusionment and burnout. Wisdom leads to hope, which triggers our ability to shape our future and transform our past. Once ignited by hope, our operational design can start creating love and meaning. It's a radical thought, I know. But we must urgently consider it if we are to address the problems we face as a human family.

Chapter 11

How hope fuels our lives

There's nothing like hope. I get creative when I get hopeful. I think most people do. Hope is what drives the development of new ideas, new solutions, all kinds of art, and other creative interpretations of what our senses tell us. Hope—not positive thinking—is why for many years I could live away from home and invest myself in others. Hope is why I was always exploring new and better ways to train others to do cataract surgery. In the end, hope is what makes us all more than machines, more than data, more than consumers, even more than individuals. Hope is like that. It gives us courage and creativity, personal strength and progressive community. It places us on a timeline towards a "real" (hoped for) future.

Sometimes we use the word "hope" to talk about wishful thinking ("I hope it won't be as bad as it looks") or positive desire ("I hope you have a good time"). But here I'm talking about hope as something far more than that. It's that attitude of confidence in what is as yet unseen. If you think of your future as an empty space, hope acts as a place holder for the amazing things you cannot yet imagine that will fill that space.

My wife and I are a good example. We made the choice to leave family and home to work in Africa without knowing much at all about what was in store for us. We felt "called" and had a sense of certainty that we could be part of something bigger than either of us. This was our hope. It was not about living out an adventure and had nothing to do with the certainty that we would make a difference. We were scared and uncertain—but we did have hope that the path we were choosing would matter. And here's the amazing thing: It turns out, it did! Hope is like that—surprising us with its rewards!

Hope drives us forward, gives us courage, and rewards us in unexpected ways. But hope by its very nature is not about certainties. I have found that it keeps us from feeling crazy as we move forward towards an uncertain future. Having hope is more like setting off on an adventure, confident that the journey will be worth it but not sure where you will end up. It is the confidence that without knowing where we are going, we will figure out how to get there. Let me emphasize this: Hope, unlike positive thinking, is not about specifics of what will be. It is only the certainty that the uncertainty will not disappoint us.

This is the difference between genuine hope and its counterfeit, positive thinking. The myth of positive thinking is that it can be used to control future outcomes with wishful thoughts. In contrast, hope is a willingness to pursue an unknown course with confidence that my divine design is exactly what I need for the unpredictable journey!

Positive thinking is good, but hope is what gives us power to meet the future. Positive thinking shows up when we have hope, but hope does not necessarily show up because of positive thinking. Hope is the sense that there is meaning in moving forward even without knowing exactly what will happen. It is neither a Pollyanna, "everything will always be okay" attitude, nor is it an Evel Knievel, "throw caution to the wind to overcome your fear" attitude. Hope endures hardship but doesn't run towards it.

Fire up the engine

What we call the "power" of positive thinking provides a momentary boost in energy. The power of hope, deeply anchored in the future, is that it fuels the engine of our divine design. It's hope that causes the fusion of body, mind, and spirit resulting in the release of enormous creative energy. Positive thinking is helpful for the moment. Hope provides energy for the long run. It sustains the parents of disabled children, holds together the lives of struggling addicts, produces perseverance through difficult times, and helps us seek lasting solutions. My wife and I have seen the power of hope in the actions of courageous patients seeking help and determined parents overcoming incredible challenges to bring us their blind child for the chance to restore their sight. They were driven by hope, not by rational, positive thinking.

This is where our Western rationalism gets in our way. We seek the facts that show us the path of least risk for greatest reward. Sometimes what we really need is to just trust our design to get us there. I realize it takes faith to believe this. But please understand what I am saying: Faith is what injects hope into our fusion engine; faith produces light and energy far beyond what we can ask or think. I am overcome with wonder every time I think of it.

We will come back to what happens when we fire up our engine in more detail in Chapter 13. First, let me share with you a little about faith and summarize what we have said so far in this book.

Chapter 12

The big picture

So far, we have learned about driving a car, wearing a hat, and igniting a fusion engine! I hope it has encouraged you to see some new possibilities for how to see yourself and this world—perhaps shining some light in the darkness around you. But the problem is, you are still bombarded daily with a slew of dehumanizing messages and actions. In our context, unmasking humanity is hard work. It takes time and courage. "Coming out" as a human being can leave you feeling doubtful, misled, and confused about where to go from here. To help with the confusion, bear with me as I review the most important ideas from Part 1.

First, remember that individualism is a myth that enslaves you to yourself and results in toxic individuality, entitlement, and narcissism. It can never truly set you free since by its nature it means life will revolve around you. Healthy individuality, on the other hand, results in a healthy self-concept, nurturing relationships, and growing community.

Second, remember that love is more than a feeling. Love fills a need within our design to belong, to be respected, and to be part of something bigger than yourself. Pursuing only the feeling of love weakens you and leads to exploitation of others while learning to receive and create love results in an endless supply of truth, beauty, and goodness, even in a damaged world.

Third, remember that your siloed achievements and possessions only produce the illusion of meaning. They never produce lasting satisfaction—only emptiness. Meaning is created by living out the hope that your divine design is exactly what you need to be significant, limitations and all. Instead of despair and loss, you begin to experience peace and joy, even in the painful experiences of life.

Finally, remember that the so called "power" of positive thinking is a myth that leads to disillusionment and burnout. Being positive about life is good, but there is no power in it. Hope—not wishful thinking—is the fuel that powers your human engine components. Hope in a tangible future ignites your divine design to create love and meaning. This produces light and life in the world around you that will last forever.

Wisdom is the key

Wisdom is the tool that unmasks the wonder of our humanity so it will shine in the dark world that surrounds us. The messages of our culture reduce us to sophisticated machines and data points. Wisdom is the Creator's perspective on all that has been made. Wisdom reminds and encourages us to be what we have been designed to be. It's accessible to all who seek it. No other creature in all the world can do what we are designed to do! We are an integral part of a creation designed to generate love and meaning.

No other creature can do that. Our Creator has designed us for this task. Wisdom is the key to discovering our divine design and understanding all our operating components.

Have a little faith

I am convinced that what we do with this information matters right now. And here is the incredible reality of it all—if it truly matters now, it will matter forever. After all, that is the nature of true meaning. The good we have done and the human beings we become using the Creator's design will last. Personally, I think this is what Jesus meant when He challenged His followers to "store up for themselves treasures in heaven." The Apostle Paul says "fire" will test what sort of work we have each done with our design to reveal that which is lasting and that which is not (1 Corinthians 3:10-15). They both wanted their followers to invest as actual contributors to the future reality of heaven and earth! Now that takes some faith!

This is the faith I'm talking about. There is no data to analyze or facts to check about future reality because, well, it is the future. But let me encourage you to take a long look at what you are as a human being. Take some time to reflect on your incredible design and see if this doesn't generate a little faith. Trust the Creator. Challenge the myths in your head and do a bit of asking, seeking, and knocking. Try taking off some of your many hats and putting on the hat of simply being human and see what that does. I'm confident that it will plant a little seed of faith. Hope grows from this seed, and with hope comes the ignition of your operational design with all its components—your own personal fusion engine! You become a source of love and meaning to those around you and your world.

Wisdom leads to a life of hope that what we do and who we are matters for eternity. Hope ignites the fusion of body, mind, and spirit as a creative engine to produce love and meaning through our lives. We become individuals in communities who actually create love and meaning in what we do and say. All this only requires that we have a little faith. And as we will discuss in Part 2, it helps to have a little plan, too!

Part 2

Remembering how to act like human beings

Glenn Strauss, M.D.

Chapter 13

How to live by divine design

So what do you get when you put together a car, a weird guy with a hat, and a fusion engine? It's not the first line of a joke—I'm being serious! What you get is one extraordinary road trip! You have a special edition "car" (your operational design as a human being) powered by a "fusion engine" (the result of ignition of your operational design by hope, as it flows into your "tank" by faith) driven by a person who knows how to optimize the car's performance on the road (wearing the hat of "Wisdom). You drive on the wheels of individuality, community, love, and meaning.

This map may help you visualize what I've said so far.

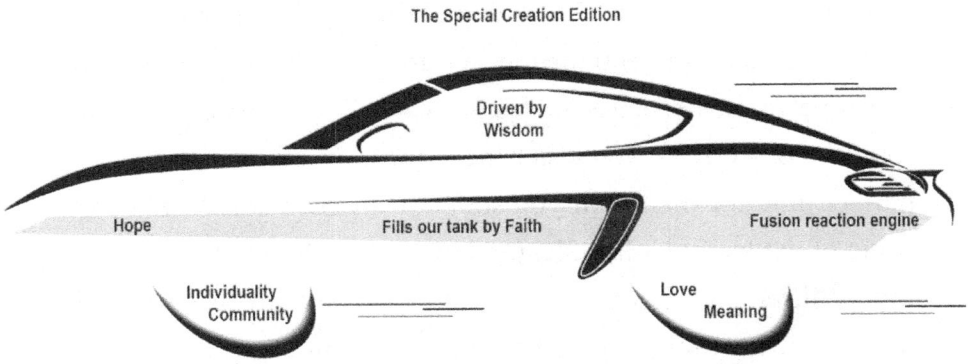

These are the fundamentals of being human. Without these fundamentals, we are going nowhere. It's time to get in the car, put on the hat, start the engine, and get the rubber on the road! But then, we still need to know where we are going. In the next few chapters, I suggest a map to follow that will lead to incredible destinations. We will learn how to build a life based on our operational design.

Let me outline the map we will use by comparing it to my surgical training strategy. When I begin with a new surgical trainee, I first teach them fundamental surgical mechanics so they will understand how things work in the microsurgical world. Then I teach them how to efficiently use these mechanics rather than trying to get them to memorize specific techniques. Finally, I teach them why they are doing the surgery in the first place (to restore vision, not just remove cataracts). They gain knowledge, learn skills, and develop the needed attitudes based on a clear definition of success.

I have refined this strategy for cataract surgery training over many years. I know learning to use your design is certainly different than learning to do eye surgery. But I believe the same learning process can work just as effectively here. I'm following roughly the same plan. You have gained essential knowledge about the fundamental "mechanics" of being human in Part 1. Now we are ready to discuss the application in Part 2—to learn specific skills and develop the needed attitudes for reaching our objective. In this case, the objective is to master the expression of our design. It's a perfect time for me to tell you some of my own stories and share some of the lessons I have learned to get you thinking about doing things differently. I can assure you that if you made it through the theoretical learning of Part 1, you are now in a great position to explore the practical applications we will discuss here.

A design-driven life

Many of you may remember the book *The Purpose-Driven Life* by Rick Warren (Zondervan Publishing, 2002). What I want to explore here is more the idea of a design-driven life. A sense of purpose is incredibly important, but I want to explain that discovering this purpose is based on an understanding of human design (specifically the divine operational design we have been studying). I believe it is this unique design that gives us purpose as human beings rather than our specific genetics and personality.

The beauty of this idea is that once you discover your operational design and how it works, the healthy functions that result will help you discover your purpose. Rather than finding a direction for your life by focusing on personal likes and dislikes or personal desires and inclinations, you recognize your purpose by experiencing your design. It turns out that the image you bear as a human being is inherently bent to produce purpose and direction since it is a reflection of the Creator of the universe. Think of it as learning to do what comes naturally—but not because it feels natural. I mean "naturally" in the sense of doing what I am designed to do at a fundamental level.

So how do we bring out the natural "best" in our design when it feels quite unnatural? What will show up in my life if I am truly acting like a human being? As I mentioned in Part 1, my life-long pursuit of Wisdom has made me a keen observer of human behavior and a student of fundamental principles. I offer some reasonable answers that have helped me in my journey, and I believe will help you in yours. The following chapters contain personal stories and examples about how to bring out the natural best in our design.

Let me summarize what I have learned before we go into detail: Our divine design, when performing at its best, enables ordinary people to act with extraordinary authority, dignity, and virtue. Our incredible design expresses itself as these three key attributes. These three qualities (authority, dignity, and virtue) blend together beautifully so that we can experience our purpose: the creation of love and meaning.

We will unpack this in the chapters to come by exploring each attribute in detail. Our design does have a dark side; this dark side can be unleashed by our egos. Instead of authority, dignity, and virtue, our operating components are perfectly capable of corruption, pompousness, and self-righteousness. We are free to respond to our egos, and when we do, all manner of pain and chaos result as we discussed in Chapters 1 and 2. The question is, is it possible to act with authority without becoming bossy or even corrupt Can we learn to act with dignity without being prideful or overtly pompous? And how can we act with virtue without becoming moralistic and self-righteous? All very good questions, indeed!

Working in parts of the world ravaged by civil war exposed me to some of the best and worst of humanity. I have seen plenty of humans behaving badly, even brutally, towards others. I have also watched in humility as some of the most unlikely people have behaved far more humanely and courageously than I. And yet, we all share the same human design, the same human DNA. Is there anything we can do to bring out the best of our humanity and not its worst? I am quite sure there is.

But what if the design is flawed?

Before I can go any further, I must take a brief detour to challenge a common religious misconception that could easily undermine your efforts to explore life by divine design. The idea I'm concerned about is referred to as "total depravity" or "original sin." Sounds grim, doesn't it! The early Church Father Augustine (354–430 C.E.) first coined the phrase to explain his view that we are "enemies of God." It explained in his mind our propensity for self-centeredness. I agree with the symptoms (our propensity to self-centeredness), but I disagree with the diagnosis (total depravity). This term is never used in the Bible, but the idea shaped much of our thinking about who we are as human beings..

Theological wars within modern Christianity have confused the issue considerably. Many churches continue to teach that our "human nature" is corrupted to the point that it is functionally and completely useless—like we are the walking dead at risk of eternal damnation simply because we are human beings. But these days, many churches have a different message. They say we are basically good and that there are no eternal consequences for any bad behavior. Modern Christianity is schizophrenic on this issue, and it has confused and divided us.

So which is it? Are we good and the victims of spiritual foul play, or are we bad and the cause of the whole mess we are in? I think the answer to who we are is in our design. We are neither intrinsically bad nor intrinsically good. I must admit that my many personal mistakes and failures seem to prove the point that we really are a hopeless mess. But I would disagree that we are totally depraved. If it were true that the image of the Creator is completely erased from humanity, we are truly beyond hope. Instead, we see in our design the evidence of a loving, giving Designer who shared His very image with us when He made us living beings. Yes, we have failed to live up to our design specifications, but the image of the Designer is still there, however damaged it may be. The engine may need some work to get it running again, but our design is basically sound!

Surely you would agree that much goodness and creativity has come from many people who are not followers of Jesus or religious in any way. Many have discovered and developed their potential as human beings without any conscious or intentional relationship with the Creator. Maybe the Designer is closer to us than we think! That said, I would be quick to add that those who don't accept or even acknowledge the Wisdom of a divine Creator are, in my view, missing out on what is needed to reach an even greater potential than they can imagine. But it doesn't mean that non-Christians are inferior human beings or that their design is fatally flawed.

All humans bear the image of the Creator whether they acknowledge it or not. The unborn and the newborn, the young and the old, the atheist, the Muslim, the Christian and the Jew, the rich and the poor, the good and the bad—all are sacred beings living within a story that is unfolding for all creation.

I return now from our little detour to the main question: How do we fully utilize the components of our divine design? What do sacred beings do? And what is the story that it tells? My intention here is to explain that no matter who you are and whether you believe my creation narrative or not, you have the tools you need to move forward as a sacred being in a story of new creation. I intend these ideas to help you begin a lifelong adventure in being human. Along the way, I fully expect you will keep running into the Creator in one way or another. But it will always be your choice what to do when that happens, whether it's a first-time encounter or a lifetime of experiences getting to know the Creator.

I invite you to use these next few chapters to help you identify specific, positive actions you can take to squeeze every drop of potential out of your divine design. I offer my experience and perspective as a tool and a guide, but in the end, this is a journey you must make as an individual. We begin in the next few chapters with consideration of the three primary functions that occur when we are utilizing our design:

- We act with authority.
- We act with dignity.
- We act with virtue.

Glenn Strauss, M.D.

Chapter 14

Expressing my divine design in using authority

When I think of the word "bossy," I can't help but picture a surgeon I once knew who loved being in charge. Once he put on his surgeon hat, he was patronizing towards the operating room staff, made disparaging suggestions, belittled patients, and was just generally gruff. I had a hard time getting past his "big man" attitude so I could provide some much-needed training for his surgical skills. Outside the operating theater, he was nice enough. Others who didn't work with him saw him as a saint, and he really did want the best for the patients. But when in charge, he became a beast. He made nurses cry, which was no small thing.

I struggled to find a way to get through to him. A change in attitude finally came one day when I asked him to examine a group of patients who had just received eye surgery. The goal was for him to tell me, without seeing the medical charts, which ones he had done and which ones I had done. We went down the row of ten patients, and he picked all the great results and even gave reasons why specific patients must have been his. Unfortunately for him, he guessed wrong in all but one of ten. I didn't need to say anything else. He has since become a much better surgeon and teacher.

It's so easy to turn a legitimate sense of confidence into a tool of pride and exploitation. Confidence in leading is a healthy result of our operational design expressing itself--it is not just the expression of an aggressive personality. The problem is that ego often gets the best of us when we're trying to lead, even when we have the best of intentions. And this inevitably leads to corruption of our natural ability. Let me suggest how we can lead without depending on our ego.

A few safeguards

I have developed some safeguards that over the years have helped me become the kind of person that others want to follow. These principles have helped me avoid the dark side of authority by aligning my "natural" instincts (embedded in my design) with Wisdom. These safeguards have helped me act with authority without becoming an ugly, controlling beast. You'd have to ask my wife, friends, and coworkers if this is, in fact, the case, but I am fairly sure they would say it's true, at least most of the time! I share the following with you as examples to consider.

Safeguard number 1 is that I try to embrace Wisdom as my primary operating system. This means I am keen to listen and learn, watch how others achieve good results, and frequently ask questions, even if the answers may seem obvious. It means I'm quick to defer to others who have reasonable or interesting ideas for how to do something.

Second, I do my best to wear only "one hat" to avoid a

fragmented lifestyle. This means I practice behaving consistently regardless of what I'm doing. I don't have a party side and a work side. As best I can, I only have one way of "being" no matter what. Frankly, it makes me a little boring, but my intention is that my actions will always carry the stamp of who I really am.

Third, I practice servant leadership. This means I try to create an upside-down hierarchy of leading with me at the bottom and others standing on my shoulders. It means I try to stay invisible even if that means I don't get the recognition I could claim.

To be clear, I don't sit down every day with my coffee and review my three goals for how to avoid being pompous. I lay these concepts out for you here so that you can consciously explore them for yourself. Maybe you are the aggressive, extroverted sort of person who needs to focus on servant leadership for now. Or maybe you need to focus on reducing the chaos of your fragmented life. Whatever the case for you, these ideas will help you express healthy authority.

But let me take it one step further. While I trust that these safeguard concepts are useful tools, I would like to paint a more detailed picture of what it looks like when I apply them to my life. Let me give you a look under the hood of the car!

Becoming a student of Wisdom

How does acting with authority look when it's an expression of my divine design and not my ego? What is the first thing I focus on? We have said that Wisdom is the primary resource for understanding and living out our operational design. For this reason, my first priority is to practice attitudes and activities that enroll me as a lifelong student of Wisdom.

Here is how I imagine I should look when participating in "Wisdom class." I would listen more and babble less. I would look for patterns in life that tell important stories about myself and others and ask questions that help me learn from those stories. I would always tell the truth.

I would be willing to change how I perceive things based on new information that helps me reframe and rethink old ideas. I would be the guy who knocks on the door of opportunity to explore new ways of doing things. I would pursue the input and support of those who have gone the path I hope to go, and I would be studying the Bible and great literature to learn how others thought about the big stories that shape us all.

It sounds a bit trite to say, but it's true: Wisdom is a journey, not a destination. Using our design to act with authority in our relationships requires considerable Wisdom, and this takes time to develop. I started the process when I was young, but you can start the class any time. The only cost is your time and attention. Get this picture of the pursuit of Wisdom in your mind and go for it!

Becoming a wise risk-taker

What about dealing with change and uncertainty? How do I get comfortable with challenge and change without grabbing the reins of control? My second priority is to practice attitudes and activities that make me a wise risk-taker.

Here is how I imagine I should look as a wise risk-taker. I

would try new ideas that express truth, beauty, or goodness without being sure they will work. I would be someone willing to fail and try again. I would be the guy who is open to criticism and quick to learn from my mistakes.

I would readily take small risks and patiently prepare for bigger risks. I would be patient with conditions and people who seem to get in my way, quick to reconcile if wronged, and slow to react defensively. I would be the guy who explores life more, savors the risks, and judges people less.

When faced with challenging options, I would be someone who chooses the simplest path, not the most complicated, even if it looks more impressive. And I would be the guy who goes for small victories, not big wins.

The reality is, we react in fear when we perceive danger. (Remember our good old "fight or flight" reaction?) Human beings are normally risk averse. This means that the activities I am suggesting here may require a step of faith to move forward. But taking a small step is often all that is needed for positive change. Jesus even said that we can "move mountains" with one small step of faith the size of a mustard seed (about $1/16^{th}$ of an inch).

We are operationally designed to take wise risks with small steps of faith. Remember, faith (not positive thinking) is what our design needs in order to be charged with hope (Chapter 11). Take some time to reflect on activities you can imagine as a wise risk-taker, and get ready to take some small steps of faith!

Glenn Strauss, M.D.

Becoming a man of integrity

For me there is one last thing I need in order to act with authority as an expression of my design, not my ego. In some ways this is fundamentally the most important. Since serving is a way of demonstrating authority without ego, I must practice attitudes and activities that help me serve others with personal integrity, humility, and consistency.

Here is how I imagine I should look when serving others with integrity. First, I would be honest with myself and others about my failures and limitations. There is no point in pretending to be something I am not, so I would find friends and activities that bring out my best and lean into that. I would be someone defined by my character, not by the situation I'm in, and I would let what I do speak for itself with no embellishment or posturing for recognition.

I would offer the best of my skills and abilities as a gift to others with no strings attached and as little pride showing as possible. I would be the guy who looks for and encourages the best in others, working for their success, and celebrating their achievements big and small. I would be patient with my own failures and the failure of others.

I would be someone who looks for the heart of a matter before reacting and make sure my service to others is not a show intended to establish superiority or power. I would be the guy looking for ways to serve from behind the scenes, seeking to highlight what is good and true and beautiful.

Remember that authority is power under control. Life is much better as an expression of your divine design than as an expression of your ego. Remember that if you allow your life to get fragmented chasing after personal rewards, you will end up burnt out and confused (Chapters 8 and 9). When controlled by ego, efforts to lead will appear self-serving, and though others may follow, you will never see their full potential or yours. The best will be hidden behind your ego. Integrity, consistency, and humility won't always put you in charge, but they will always allow you to act with healthy authority.

A story of beautiful leadership

Let me end this chapter with a story to illustrate some of these points. This is the story of a young woman who lived in a rather remote village in Liberia. People listened to her. Even the men listened though she had to pretend she was not actually offering advice. She was a mobilizer and a doer when things needed to get done. This young lady heard of an eye screening I was doing some distance from her village and succeeded in getting much of the village to come, including quite a few I could really help! She worked quietly in the background making sure everyone was taken care of, including the children.

On the day of surgery, there she was again, this time encouraging those who were having surgery, and going to get a bit of food for family members who were waiting. I came up to her and through a translator I said, "I know why all these patients are here today." She looked up a bit surprised that I had even noticed her at all. I said, "They are here because of you!" I'll never forget her smile. She became a member of the eye team, and I'm sure that now long after the eye team has gone, she continues to be an effective leader.

Your operational design is ideally suited to allow you to act with authority in your sphere of influence and beyond. Healthy and effective authority comes out of those who are learners, who take wise risks, and who serve with integrity. Practicing these skills makes it far less likely that your ego will take over. With a bit of time and practice, you will look around and notice that others are not so much following you as they are growing and enjoying being their best.

Chapter 15

Expressing my divine design through a life of dignity

I remember meeting the king of the Voodoo religion in Benin one afternoon. I don't mean this to sound like we were meeting for a cup of coffee to discuss the latest ballgame. It was quite a bit more serious than that. He had his shaman with him and was obviously trying to avoid showing his worry about his bad eyesight. He came to find out if he had cataracts and if they could be removed so he could see better. For him it was a matter of life and death. If anyone in his tribe knew he couldn't see, he could be dethroned—and apparently that was not a pretty thing.

He was puffed up, standing tall, dressed to kill (I was really hoping not literally), and with a look of disdain for all of us mere mortals. No one else was allowed in the room. Frankly, I think he was so full of himself there was just no room for anyone else. Even worse, his inflated ego seemed to switch on my ego. I had to pause and push down the urge to go full surgeon on him.

My eye team (except for my brave wife) had all disappeared, terrified that he might curse someone if he felt threatened or dishonored. I cautiously examined his eyes. He sent his shaman out of the room so I could explain his condition to him and the procedure needed to fix it. I was respectful and as honoring of his position as I could be, but maybe I explained a little too much about the "cutting on his eyeball" part. I couldn't help myself. I'm sorry to say, he never came back.

It's easy to turn a legitimate sense of importance as human beings into an inflated sense of self-importance. A sense of our value and the importance of being human is appropriate and constructive (that's the name of this book, after all!). But if ego gets the best of us, the beauty of our design gets distorted. Just like "the beast" hungering for control, another pretentious beast shows up when an unchecked ego infects our natural sense of value. This inevitably leads to narcissistic self-importance that corrupts our "natural" human function to act with dignity. Self-importance is always at the expense of the importance of others. It is always destructive. It reeks of shame and disgrace. It's anything but dignified. Let me suggest how to display dignity without self-importance.

A few safeguards for avoiding self-importance

I have developed some personal safeguards that have helped me over the years to act with dignity and self-respect in my relationships while avoiding self-importance. These principles have given me confidence and poise talking to presidents, gurus, ambassadors, and billionaires. But they have also allowed me to walk with the poor and disempowered as fellow human beings and walk through difficult times in my own life with humility rather than resentment.

You may associate the idea of dignity with the elite and the powerful. You may think of it as being a bit stuffy, like being the King or Queen of England. But in fact, dignity is about demonstrating what we hold in common as human beings. It's about honoring our divine design. I need certain safeguards to remind me that we are all in this together, united by a common heritage and called to a noble purpose.

Safeguard number 1 is that I try to embrace humility as my primary attitude towards life and others. This of course is easier said than done. It means I choose to view my design as a gift, not a right. I embrace the fact that I have a design the same as everyone else around me. I delight in reflecting the importance of a Designer rather than my own importance. I love the quote from Rick Warren: "Humility is not thinking less of yourself. It is thinking of yourself less."

Second, I do my best to be unassuming and unpretentious. This means I spend a lot more time trying to understand than demanding to be understood. I apply the brakes to my natural compulsion for vindication and allow my actions to speak for themselves. Instead of striking out on my own to fix problems, I value the perspective of others and work collaboratively as much as possible.

Third, I practice the "golden rule." You remember this one: "Do unto others as you would have them do unto you." It's still timely advice and goes a long way towards making sure you don't look like a two-year-old pouting on the floor when you don't get your way. Not much dignity in that! Dignity comes with maturity, and maturity values and respects others.

This brings us back to the challenge of finding ways to live out these personal safeguards. It helps me to imagine specific behavior patterns that paint the picture of a dignified life. Let's take another look under the hood of my car!

Taking responsibility for myself

How does acting with dignity look when it's an expression of my divine design and not my ego? The first thing I must remember is that dignity shows up when I take responsibility for what I do. It may be a failure, or it may be a great success, but either way, when I own what I do, I take a step towards personal dignity.

The problem is, most of us believe that many of our problems are someone else's fault. It's so easy to fall into this trap because our pride does not want to show any weakness. Any sense of personal value or dignity disappears when we make others responsible for our problems. If I want to express the dignity of my design without the influence of my pride, my priority is to practice attitudes and activities that ensure I take responsibility for myself.

Here is how I imagine that should look. I would stay active so that I could be alert and ready to address the challenges of the day. I would focus on the simple things for which I can take responsibility and, as much as possible, avoid unnecessary complexity. I would avoid trivializing the problems and hurts of others.

I would be the guy who is content with what I have but takes the initiative to get what is needed if anything is lacking. I would be someone who takes time to relish the beauty of creation and the wonder of life and avoids prolonged escape from reality in whatever form that might take.

I would be someone who avoids making choices I know I will regret and never make excuses when I make the wrong choices. I would spend less time defending my intentions and more time looking for how I could improve.

Dignity does not mean prowess or status. It means taking personal responsibility for my actions. This is a tough pill to swallow when everyone else is making excuses. But in the end, healthy dignity will be its own reward.

Doing life gracefully

Life is full of undignified moments, awkward silences, and foolish mistakes. We all have our faults and limitations that we may want to hide. But in reality, these limitations are usually there for a reason. To act with dignity my second priority is to do life gracefully within my personal limits.

Here's how I imagine I should look gracefully navigating life's challenges. I would own my limitations as well as my strengths and establish healthy boundaries for use of my time and resources. I would be the guy who stops and asks for help when needed. I would ask for directions when I don't know where I'm going.

I would be someone who laughs at the paradoxes of life. In fact, I would be the sort of person who just laughs more! I would learn how to focus on small successes even when failure has occurred. I would be the guy with a playful approach to problem-solving, anticipating the good that will come from it but never pretending bad is good. I would be someone who looks for experiences that make me feel small but not devalued, like standing on a mountain, looking at the grandeur of the world.

I would be someone who accepts constructive criticism and pushes back on dishonesty, destructive accusations, and harsh words. I would offer only as much direction to others as is absolutely necessary to nudge thinking towards the best possible outcomes. I would be someone who is more concerned about the success of a project than who gets the credit for it.

Life is messy, but we can live with dignity in it by embracing our limitations gracefully and extending this same grace to others. Our pride wants us to hide our faults, but in the end, our faults will show through looking far less dignified than if we had just embraced them to begin with.

Extending myself within a healthy community

For me, there is one other thing I need to do to display the dignity of my design. I need to invest myself in others who are willing to invest themselves in me. This is hard to do given the imperfections we all have. But I believe I must make it a priority to find a community that brings out our best. There is something humbling, and at the same time affirming, about the effect of a healthy community on us. It is the setting in which we feel honor and dignity the most. The third thing I must do to express the dignity of my divine design is to find and extend myself within a healthy community.

Here's how I imagine I would look finding and engaging with

such a community. I would look for people who are honest with themselves and with each other about life. I would be someone who takes the time to listen to those who appear to be on the fringe, as well as to those who appear to be in charge. I would watch what people do and not just what they say.

I would be someone who explores small opportunities to engage and serve, doing the best I can to align my personal skills and abilities with the needs and goals of the community. I would be the guy who encourages cooperation and unity, but I would not fear being disruptive if needed for conscience's sake or for the greater good. I would expect a healthy community to accept disruption from time to time to stay healthy. I would be someone who finishes well.

I would be someone who draws out the heart and mind of others. I would receive appreciation gracefully and sincerely offer appreciation to others. I would work to reduce awkwardness, inequality, and manipulation in relationships.

Let me just say up front that there is no such thing as a perfect community—but there is such a thing as a healthy community. Signs of health usually include diversity of age and background, a shared vision for life and well-being, and a pattern of open communication, shared responsibility, and shared authority. I would bet that there are not many readers who have ever experienced a healthy community. We live in a culture of divisiveness and individualism, not community. As a whole, we experience social networks and electronic "friending" much more than genuine society and neighbors. But we can each be part of a solution to these problems.

Even in the best of conditions, community is hard to achieve. The good news is that there are healthy communities around if you look. They may not be found in the biggest churches or among the country club crowd or the well-to-do. You may or may not find it with your biological family. It might just be that small group of people around you, sharing life together, attracted to each other by a common vision for something more than what our culture seems to offer. Regardless of where you find it, you cannot function fully without it. And the reality is, it cannot function fully without you.

A story of simple dignity

Let me end this chapter with another story to illustrate some of these points. I remember learning about dignity one afternoon when my wife and I were at a home in Benin, paying a visit to a child I had operated on a few weeks previously. The father was a tailor and the mother worked in the market selling her husband's goods. I was bringing some glasses for their little girl. As we approached their home, she ran out to meet us and playfully tugged at my wife's dress, wanting her to come quickly to see her new room. Wow, we did love her smile! The parents were gracious and welcoming, and they were all dressed in what must have been some of his finest tailored clothes.

What I haven't told you is that their "home" was four sheets of corrugated metal leaning together, literally on top of a garbage dump. The little girl's "room" was a part of the dirt floor where she played with trash turned into treasures. The family behaved with such dignity and grace that as far as we were concerned, we were talking to the president and first lady of the country (who in fact, we had just met the previous week). We gave the little girl her glasses. They gave us a new vision of what the dignity of being human looks like.

The components of your operational design (body, mind, and spirit) are ideally suited to display dignity and self-respect. Healthy dignity seems to naturally flow from those who use their design to take responsibility for themselves, gracefully operate within their limitations, and extend themselves constructively within a healthy community. Practicing these skills makes it far less likely that your ego will take over. With a bit of time, you will look around and notice that there are others not only enjoying you, but also feeling better about themselves when they are around you. Dignity is contagious!

Glenn Strauss, M.D.

Chapter 16

Expressing my divine design through a life of virtue

I met with a group of missionaries one afternoon after a long day in the operating theater. They were there at my invitation to discuss ways we might be able to work together. I made sure they were received as honored guests. As we enjoyed some light refreshments, our discussion seemed to gradually become a test. Did I have the right answers to their questions about evangelism, the Bible, a personal relationship with God? I guess I didn't. They seemed a bit put out by my unconventional thinking and my ideas about how to put those we were called to serve above our religious agendas to "save" them. No matter what I said they seemed to have figured out how to always be right. The implications were clear—I was not up to their standards. There was no chance of working with them. I felt defeated by "good" theology and "good" intentions.

We are designed with a sense of right and wrong. For most people, conscience is a reliable moral guide. But it's surprisingly easy to turn our personal convictions into a belief that I personally must set the moral standards for the whole world. An appropriate sense of right and wrong and the ability to act selflessly are a normal expression of our divine design. But once again, ego can get the best of us, corrupting our proper functions. Like "the ugly beasts" of narcissism or pretentiousness perverting healthy authority and self-respect, unchecked ego can turn healthy virtue into a sanctimonious display of self-righteousness. Ego can turn my conscience and beliefs into a weapon used to dominate others. Allow me to suggest how to act with virtue without becoming self-righteous.

A few safeguards against self-righteousness

Virtue is an antiquated if not negative word these days. It is associated with hypocritical Christians and self-righteous pride. But virtue is about demonstrating the goodness of life. It is about properly valuing the divine design that we all share. I need certain safeguards to help me express virtue without becoming self-righteous and judgmental. Over many years, these safeguards have gradually aligned my instincts with Wisdom. I have discovered that healthy virtue adds a sort of personal beauty and wholeness to my life when combined with healthy expressions of authority and dignity. The gracefulness of virtue is not easy to express. But here are some examples of the safeguards I use to hopefully get you started.

Safeguard number 1 is that I embrace purity as a lifestyle. The idea of purity is a bit hard to define. The word sounds prudish or maybe old-fashioned, out of place in today's sexually obsessed world. What I mean by a lifestyle of purity is staying focused on the fundamentals of wholeness, decency, honor, and transparency as a human being—what it means to be a "beautiful person." A lifestyle of purity means I avoid many of today's culturally acceptable activities, not so much because they are "bad" but because of how they affect me—activities that make me less than beautiful. They turn me into something I am not. In general, choosing purity means making choices that give value to my life and the lives of others rather than what makes me happy.

Second, I choose to be unassuming. I study the whole picture surrounding events in life, not just isolated facts or experiences. I stay conscious of the fact that there is a context for everything that happens. Without context, I can make most anything others do sound wrong, and without transparency revealing my motives, I can make most anything I do seem right! To be unassuming requires me to properly understand my own behaviors and biases before I question the behavior and agendas of others. Instead of assuming bad intentions, I use discernment to try to see how the choices of others produce consequences that could have been avoided if different choices were made. Looking at the whole picture does not mean making excuses for bad behavior or being naive, but it does mean I can humbly encourage good choices with an awareness of the complexity of life.

Third, I employ my individuality as a gift, not a right. This means that in marriage, in friendships, at work, and at play I do not demand my rights. Instead, I enjoy using my individuality to produce life and love around me as best I can. Sometimes this means standing against things that dehumanize and devalue my life or the life of others. Sometimes this takes courage, and yes, sometimes it will cost me. But it does not mean that my rights trump yours. It means I use my rights, my individuality, as a tool for good.

This brings us back once again to the challenge of how to live out these safeguards. Just like our discussion on acting with authority and dignity, let me share an action plan and a few ideas for specific patterns of behavior that paint the picture of virtue. Once again, my examples are just a starting point to get your own imagination going.

Protecting my thought life

We have a massive problem in our culture with culturally acceptable narcissism. We have (almost) made self-centeredness a virtue! There is no end to the dehumanizing trash being displayed in the name of freedom of expression. Personal virtue, it seems, is lost in the shadows between freedom of choice and rampant decadence. I am convinced that this is a battle won or lost in the mind. If I want to live a virtuous life, my first priority must be to control and protect my own thought life.

Here's how I imagine that should look in my life. Rather than dwelling on images, ideas, and words that lead down negative and dehumanizing paths, I would do all I can to stop destructive thought pathways from forming by focusing on what is good, true, or positive. I would acknowledge the reality of evil, but do not let it define my worldview. I would do the best I can to focus on what is beautiful in others instead of only noticing their faults.

I would become a careful observer of all sides of life, both the good and the bad. I would be someone who focuses on ideas and patterns that I see and hear, rather than being swayed by the personal agendas or vendettas of others. I would be the guy who is open to opinions but avoid those who are using their agendas to hurt others. I would limit my exposure to those who seem intent on hatred and violence. I would read literature that helps me think critically and expansively.

I would be careful of bias in my own thinking. I would test my ideas by interacting with peers in thoughtful conversations and by spending time meditating on the life and messages of Jesus. I would be someone who uses reading and experiences to explore new ideas, but check myself against the Wisdom of those who are older and wiser before assuming new directions are good.

Our minds are perhaps our greatest asset, but one of the most vulnerable to damage. The only check on your thought life is what you yourself provide. No one can hear your thoughts but you. No one can control your thoughts but you. Virtue is an expression of your divine design that begins with healthy thinking.

Projecting an image of well-being

Virtue could also be viewed as the projection of a healthy self-image. Human beings have remarkable brains for storing information both consciously and unconsciously. As the center of our reactions and behaviors, our brains also project an image of our inner state through our physical body. In psychiatry they call it our affect. Parents call it having an attitude. Sometimes we refer to it as body language, and mystics sometimes refer to it as our aura. We all project a certain image that is often just a display of our own egos. My point is, I believe we are designed to display an image of virtue. So how do we go about expressing ourselves in a way that displays the beauty of virtue? I believe it is by practicing attitudes and activities that project an image of wholeness and well-being.

Here's how I imagine that should look. I would be honest in my communication, with a clarity that comes from being comfortable with my own limitations. I would be someone who makes appropriate eye contact and engages fully and sincerely with others. I would not be the guy who becomes defensive when challenged.

I would be a peacemaker. I would be someone who acts as a problem solver, not a whiner or complainer. I would be the guy who speaks appropriate words of affirmation and encouragement into the lives of others and who offers constructive criticism at the right time, in the right place, and with the right attitude. I would gracefully receive thanks and honor from others.

I would celebrate the success of others. I would be someone who forgives without expecting repentance and who looks for redemptive pathways in relationships. I would respect my own boundaries as well as the space and time of others. I would be inclusive, not exclusive.

Projecting an image of power, control, or pride only produces isolation. Projecting an image of virtue draws people in. It expresses and reinforces the best and the most beautiful aspects of our design.

Learning to be a blessing

For me there is one last thing I need to do to keep my ego out of the picture. The wholeness, decency, honor, and transparency expressed in virtue is intended for good, not evil. Virtue produces a sort of fruit that is enjoyable and encouraging for others to eat. I like to use the word "blessing" to describe this fruit even though it has a bit of a religious sound to it. The third thing I must do to express the virtue of my design is to practice attitudes and activities that ensure I am a blessing.

Here's how I imagine that should look in my life. I would use my personal abilities, resources, and my social network to help others succeed, working as much as possible behind the scenes so others won't ever know about it. In times of challenge for my friends and family, I would be the shoulders to stand on for moving forward, not just a shoulder to lean on for rest.

I would work on discovering and encouraging the conditions and activities that unite us as human beings rather than dividing us. I would be someone who celebrates with those who have given their best regardless of the outcome and grieves with those who experience failure or loss. I would be the guy who encourages greatness and life in others, not just happiness.

I would be someone who gives practical resources and opportunities to others, not just words of encouragement. Whenever possible, I would be the guy who makes hope tangible, not mere wishful thinking. I would be someone who builds a legacy of truth, goodness, and beauty in my family, my community, and my business.

The beauty of virtue shines brightest when we are a blessing to others rather than a critic. This is not easy for us to do in our culture. It often takes people by surprise. We are designed to express virtue as blessing, not self-righteousness. To do so we must protect our thought lives and create an image of well-being, but we must also learn to be a surprising experience of life and blessing in someone's day.

A story of a virtuous life

Frankly, it's difficult to come up with a lot of examples of virtuous living in our culture. My wife certainly fits the description, but I will spare her the embarrassment of carrying on about my "Proverbs 31 woman"! (Look it up—she fits the description of Proverbs 31:10–31.) Fortunately for her, another story comes to mind. On my first trip to Africa, I met an ophthalmic nurse who obviously cared deeply about the well-being of his patients. We, as health care providers, were all supposed to care, but like most of the team, we did not speak the tribal languages needed to communicate this directly to our patients. For this we had a team of translators. What I discovered was that this extraordinary nurse cared for our patients by caring for our team of translators.

He had a gentlemanly way of pushing the translator team to be their best. He was clear in his expectations and made them feel their job was important. He pointed out "that surgeon" (pointing to me), who just had to do his job for a few minutes with each patient, while they had to work for hours to make sure our patients felt secure and comfortable. He included them as care providers and provided technical training to many of them. He was honest when he saw mistakes but celebrated the successes of each team member. He would not accept halfhearted efforts from anyone, but seemed infinitely patient when his team was giving its best. He cared enough to know how that could look in each individual on the team.

He was patient with me as well and always seemed to think that I could get the "job" done best by receiving constructive feedback about my results. Thanks to his sincerity and trustworthiness, I was happy to receive it. Providing quality surgical care in harsh conditions and surrounded by watching donors, fearful patients, and "slightly" inflated egos of care providers was no small trick. Yet he managed it all, often working in the background to ensure success. For him, there were no shortcuts, no grand press releases, just hard work to get the job done well. Many of those translators went on to become highly skilled care providers in their own countries, reflecting in their own lives the virtue he demonstrated. He was a blessing to them, and they became a blessing to others.

With my deepest gratitude but little credit for the huge impact of his work, he retired to be a preacher in small, largely ignored churches in the UK. By the way, my wife carried on this legacy, leading the team of translators as a blessing for years after he left. I wish the blind everywhere had champions like the two of them.

Your operational design is ideally suited for this same kind of virtuous living. It's demonstrated by clear thinking, projecting well-being, and by the blessing you become to others. Practicing these skills makes it far less likely that your ego will take over as you express the virtue of your design. And as you begin to act with virtue, you will discover that your impact on others is far out of proportion to what you might think is possible. Over time, you will notice that those around you are giving more than they are receiving. You will see others around you being a blessing. Like authority and dignity, virtue is contagious.

What now?

I realize I've given you a lot to take in. I think you would agree that nothing is difficult about the information itself, but I know there is quite a bit to digest. In the end, it's all just words and ideas that I hope will make it easier for you to imagine a picture of yourself being human in the fullest sense.

I've let you take a look under the hood of my car as honestly as I can and tried to arrange my thoughts like pieces of a puzzle so you can begin assembling a complete picture of your own. Just let it settle a bit in your mind. There are no checklists for self-improvement here, nor is there any presumption that these ideas are just what you need to enhance your life. These ideas may or may not be useful to you right now. But over time any Wisdom in my words may start to illuminate a way forward.

To get the most out of your reading, I would suggest you select one or two ideas that grab your attention. Choose ideas that seem like they might be enjoyable or satisfying. Don't start with a list of all the bad qualities you want to fix!

Once you have selected one or two ideas, then consider what you will actually do to incorporate the ideas into your own life. Make sure you develop a realistic "how to" plan that is doable in one to two months. In a few sentences, write down a clear idea of what you want to achieve and how you will know you have achieved it. Then, run it past a few people you trust. That's it. Seriously—that's all it takes to start a process that will produce some incredibly good things in your life. In effect, this process will become your action plan for expressing your divine design one step at a time. And I assure you, just one small change can produce impressive results.

When you're ready to share your action plan, try a conversation with a trusted companion that goes something like this: "I want to try something new for a change. I've got some ideas on how to do it. Want to help me figure it out?" A conversation like this is incredibly easy and generally well received. Don't be concerned if it's awkward at first. Just reassure them that you really do value their input, however simple it may be.

I can tell you from years spent in training others, this process is not a guarantee, but it gives you the best chance of success. It boils down to creating a simple action plan: Be as clear as possible about what you want to do in the long term, formulate a simple, short-term plan for how to get it done, and discuss a few practical steps with others who can act as your observers and encouragers. Simple. Powerful. Effective! It does take some practice and effort to get started. But then change always does.

What am I sure of

What I am sure of is this: Every human being is designed to express healthy authority, dignity, and virtue in our world. These functions are a vital part of our mandate to reflect the image of our Creator. The trick for us is leaning into our human design rather than creating a pile of frustrating goals and expectations. As these pieces come together, there is a sort of rhythm to life that I think you will find resonating deeply within you. When you start to feel that resonance, you know your divine engine is powered up!

So get your engine running and head out on the highway (sorry, couldn't resist a little "Born to Be Wild" theme music here), because here's the thing—once you get comfortable with your divine, operational design, it's time to get a little uncomfortable again. As you develop skills to act with authority, dignity, and virtue, it's time to go a little wild and start creating! Remember from Chapters 6–9 that the creation of love and meaning are the primary purpose for our design reflecting the Creator. Now we need to consider how this works. This is a chance for you to tell a new story with your life as you learn to express your divine design.

Perhaps it's helpful to provide a short summary to build some momentum for your next steps. Here's what we have said so far in Chapters 14–16:

> My divine operational design as a human being is built to:
> o   Act with authority.
> o   Act with dignity.
> o   Act with virtue.
>
> Unchecked ego (self-focus) corrupts each of these functions.
> o   Authority is corrupted by ego to look like bossiness and manipulation.
> o   Dignity is corrupted by ego to look like pompousness and narcissism.
> o   Virtue is corrupted by ego to look like self-righteousness and sanctimonious moralism.
>
> Purposefully taking action interrupts the corrupting

influence of ego and enables me to function according to my human design. These actions can be described in the following groups or clusters of behavior:
1. To act with authority, I must choose to:
   a. Be a lifelong student of Wisdom.
   b. Be a wise risk-taker.
   c. Serve others with integrity.
2. To act with dignity, I must choose to:
   a. Take responsibility for myself.
   b. Operate gracefully within my human and personal limitations.
   c. Extend myself within a healthy community.
6. To act with virtue, I must choose to:
   a. Control and protect my thought life.
   b. Project an image of wholeness and well-being to others.
   c. Be a blessing.

When you are ready, read on to see how to become the creator you were designed to be!

Glenn Strauss, M.D.

Chapter 17

How to be a creator of love and meaning

One of the great joys of my career in missions was working with a particular ophthalmic theater sister from New Zealand (for those of us in the U.S., "theater" means operating room and "sister" means nurse). At first glance she seemed such a small, fragile thing. You would never know she had spent years working in the Congo patching up rebel forces at a mission hospital in the bush. She didn't talk much about it. In fact, she didn't talk much about herself in general. She could be a bit stern and directive and was not really the warm, huggy type. She often accused me of being a "slacker" for only getting twenty cases done instead of thirty in a day or fussed at me for reaching over to take an instrument off "her" tray or using too many of "her" supplies. The twinkle in her eye told me she would only settle for my best, and she seemed to know what "my best" was, even when I forgot. What was interesting to me was that everyone absolutely loved her. Something just came out of her as we led the operating theater team together, which generated a loving atmosphere for all of us.

She developed Parkinson's disease, and on the last day we

worked together, I looked up to find she had stepped out of her manager role so we could work side-by-side as surgeon and scrub nurse. Our eyes met over our surgical masks, but I didn't say anything. The whole room seemed to pause to watch. The cataract surgery took about five minutes, and afterwards she said just a bit awkwardly to the whole team, "This is what love is like. I just had to do it one more time." It makes me cry to this day. This was a moment when love was created for us all.

I am happy to tell you that after she left the mission field, she met the love of her life, married, and now lives in New Zealand with dozens of nieces and nephews, all bringing her great joy. I'm sure she is still creating love for those around her.

Our design is wired to produce love

The reality is that love never comes easily or cheaply, but it's never beyond our ability because it's built into our design. Let me refresh your memory from Chapter 7 about a few things we must do to turn on the components of our divine design to express the love of the Designer. First, to create love, we must trust that our divine design is built to generate love. It takes a bit of faith, but once we accept the possibility of being the expression of a loving Designer, our ability to create love starts to make sense. We are actually recreating what is expressed in our design by our Designer. Once we know what we are looking for, we can see it in others and in ourselves. It's like the surprise we get when putting on a good pair of glasses for the first time—the trees have leaves; there really are words on those road signs at night! Once we look at ourselves and the world through the eyes of divine design, we can see love almost everywhere, even in the darkness of the world around us.

Second, remember that love is not something we "possess." It's not an expression of warmth that certain people have and others don't. Love is something created by anyone using their divine design to experience the journey of life with others. This does not mean that all functions of our design must operate perfectly—they never will! But it does mean that they must at least be functioning, however imperfectly. Creating love assumes our divine design is functioning with authority, dignity, and virtue. In other words, if there is no virtue in my life, I cannot create love. If there is no dignity, no love. No authority? Again, no love. You get the picture.

Third, we must accept the fact that generating love costs us something. For me as a unique human being, the cost is the price of my ego. The reason for this is simple: I must give away what I create to express love. It has been said, "We can give without loving, but we cannot love without giving." But remember, we can create without using up any resources. Love is not self-destructive. Quite the opposite. When love is created out of our design, we are never used up. We are expanded and strengthened!

The nuts and bolts of love

In the end, it comes down to the daily choices I make. Let me describe the nuts and bolts of love building as I imagine them for my life. I would call a friend for no reason other than to say I'm thinking about them. I might send an encouraging note or text for no particular reason. I might surprise someone with something good. I would be someone who gives generously.

I would give my face the freedom to say what my heart feels. I would do more than what others ask or expect. I would be the guy who comes alongside someone who seems overwhelmed or a little lost in a crowd. I might talk with a friend about something that matters deeply to me and take time to listen to what matters to them. I would be someone who takes time for my family so I can really see how they are doing and experience a little bit of their life with them.

I would be someone who takes time to offer kindness in secret. I might make a special meal for someone and eat it with them unhurried and undistracted. I would open my home to others even if it's inconvenient for me. I would extend myself in ways that demonstrate the importance of others, even people I do not know. I would be someone who serves honorably and faithfully, even if I get no credit.

I have a lot more suggestions, but these few are intended to get you thinking a little more creatively than just sending a get-well card or flowers to express love. To be clear, just doing loving things may make you feel good temporarily but will not necessarily create love. It takes full engagement of body, mind, and spirit energized by hope to create love. I say this not to discourage you but to keep you from getting frustrated and quitting if you try these things and nothing "magic" seems to happen. Keep trying! Remember, it takes time to align your attitudes with your actions and opportunities to love. It takes faith to trust your design and hope that you can recreate the Designer's love.

Counting the cost of creating love

Once you start down this path of creating love, you will soon discover that the cost gradually increases. To begin with, there is often what could be called a "production cost" for creating love—a bit of time to write a note or the cost to prepare a meal, money given to a friend in need or to a support a worthy cause. But I warn you that there will also be a personal cost as time goes on. Giving your time and energy will start to feel like loss, like true sacrifice, like being spent. I warn you about this because this is not what we expect love to feel like! But guess what—that feeling of loss is actually the release of your own ego. It's like the good "burn" you get from hard exercise. Once the burn is gone, you have the high it produces. The cost of the ego being emptied also produces a good "burn" and its own high—the sense of completeness, peace, and satisfaction that comes with creating love.

Let me illustrate with a deeply moving story my colleague Dr. Steven Arrowsmith, a fellow missionary surgeon, has allowed me to share:

> My wife and I attended the Urbana Missions Conference years ago with thousands of students considering life as a missionary as an intense exposure of what missions was all about. One person in particular had riveted my wife Jan's attention. She was a feisty Irish doctor who had single-handedly established a hospital and nursing school responsible for a population of over one million in the bush of the Belgian Congo. Later, she endured dark times as independence came violently to Zaire. Her name was Helen Roseveare. Jan

was inspired, and vowed that she, too, would one day be a woman missionary doctor in Africa, just like Helen.

Years later, we were dumbfounded to learn that we would be at a missions meeting with Helen as our cottage-mate. She had heard about our recent near-death experience in our mission assignment, and in the evenings after the conference sessions, she frankly but gently counseled us. She told us about things she had experienced that weren't in any of her books.

During Zaire's Simba rebellion, she had been captured and held by rebels for several months. She was imprisoned with a group of Belgian nuns, one of whom was particularly beautiful. And so, nearly every night, their captors lined up to rape this unfortunate woman. Very soon she seemed to simply lose her life-spark, withdrawn into a shell, something less than a person. The Mother Superior came to Helen and begged her to "say something" as a doctor to the young woman before she died of a crushed spirit. Helen had no clue what to say. For lack of anything better to say, she came up with a line that, even to Helen, sounded lame: "Maybe God is allowing this to happen to you so that it won't happen to the rest of us."

Somehow, this struck a chord in the woman's mind, and she seemed renewed enough to go on living. She was protecting her sisters by enduring this unimaginable abuse. Helen was relieved and a bit amazed that her advice had worked. Then that evening, the nightly ritual began again. A drunken rebel staggered in and demanded to know where the young nun was. Suddenly Helen heard a voice, a voice she knew to be God's, that didn't say, "Don't worry, I've got this," not, "Hang on a second, and I will save the day." No, the voice said, "Hey, Helen, you know that line you used on this poor nun here? Were you serious? Did you really mean what you were saying about protecting others? If so . . ." Then

Helen understood that it was one thing to claim some sappy spiritual insight, and another to practice the sacrificial Love that made it real. Her young colleague needed protection, or she was going to die. So, Helen jumped up and said, "Hey, you! Over here! Why don't you come take me instead?!"

For the nun, Helen had provided the ability to see beyond her current crisis, to be reminded that there was an unseen realm that operated by different rules, but that ultimately held out her hope and context for being. This had given her what she needed to go on at that moment in that place, without being rescued, but rather reframed. But the same look at reality pushed Helen to make an unimaginable decision to show love to her in a most costly way. Her willingness to trust in God's love for her was so unwavering that her understanding of the transcendent strength and power of this love moved her to volunteer for sexual assault.

Love we create is rarely this dramatic or costly, but it proves to be just as powerful. Love created out of the image of the Creator of our divine design is not some grand gesture. It's a simple but profound expression of the beauty of the Designer. We need only to take action, accept the cost, make some simple choices, and let our design do the rest.

How to create meaning

One Sunday I was teaching at a small church that met at a youth campground. There was a new lady in the group that day. She was older, neatly dressed, with well-kept, gray hair. She seemed intently interested in what I was teaching from the book of James. Her eyes betrayed a sense that she was somehow intensely interested in my story as well.

After the service, she came up to me, asked what I liked about the church, and seemed to be leading up to something. I was in a bit of a rush to get home and a little distracted since my wife was not well. (In fact, she had not been well for some time.) But something about her face and eyes told me I needed to listen. She held up her finger and said as she pointed towards me, "Young man (I was thirty-something at the time), God has something very special He wants to do with your life." And that was that. She turned and left. I asked who she was and found out that she was just in from the mission field for a short visit.

Turns out she had been a leader in missions for fifty years. She had been widowed quite young and since then specialized in developing leaders for missions. She came to my office a few weeks later, supposedly for an eye examination. Our conversation quickly turned to the idea of missionary service, and she wasted no time in inviting me on what was to be my first missionary trip. As it turns out, my job was to carry her books. I still remember how meaningful that simple job was as I traveled around the Philippines. There was more meaning in it than many other "important" jobs I have done over the years. I discovered later that I had become one of her five "sons" as she called us. Thirty years later, I am still doing missions because of the profoundly meaningful moments she created for me to enjoy.

It can be fairly easy to create opportunities for meaningful experiences by doing very simple things at the right time and in the right way. Let me remind you of a few specific concepts we discussed in Chapter 9 about using our operational design to create opportunities for meaning and significance— even in the seemingly mundane things of life. I list a few ideas here just as an encouragement to help you start formulating a plan.

Our design is wired to produce meaning

I know it may be a little late to ask, but do you know what it means to create meaning? I think it's an important question because we normally think of events or words that are meaningful to us. We all know what that means. But the idea that meaning is something caused by us is something different. To wrap my head around it, I begin with the idea that my divine design is built to engage in the world around me. I am a bit of an introvert so for me this takes faith and courage. I accept that I don't just experience the world, it experiences me, and I have a responsibility to bring meaning to it. Once I accept that I am designed for this purpose, I become more intentional about watching for opportunities, taking risks, and owning my responsibility.

I must also accept that meaning can only be created as I journey with others. Healthy relationships are the shortest path to meaningful experiences. All the components of my design (body, mind, and spirit) must be operating, however imperfectly, to express authority, dignity, and virtue in my relationships with others. The opportunities to bring meaning to even simple experiences grow out of our ability to live well.

Finally, I must live as if the creation of meaning is my greatest privilege. By using my divine design, I bring meaning to what I do and say. I bring meaning from my individuality to the love I create and to the communities in which I engage. I do that—not fate, not others, not even God. (I know my Christian friends may be shaking their heads about now.) The Creator has designed us all to bear His image so that we can bring meaning and significance into our world! It's truly an incredible privilege.

The nuts and bolts of creating meaning in life

Once again, creating meaning comes down to the daily choices I make. Let me describe the nuts and bolts I imagine using to construct meaning with my life. I would be the guy who asks lots of questions and thoughtfully and constructively challenges conventions I would be someone who tries to find new ways to look at old problems, and I would be bold in applying new solutions even though they might fail. I would focus on the potentially profound effects of simple actions. I would keep reminding people about what really matters.

I would be someone who works and lives supportively with others, not just around them, using every opportunity to share experiences. I might take time for a walk or to watch the sunset with someone. I would watch children playing and really listen for the joy in their laughter. I would wade into the messiness of life with others and share my observations as a fellow human being with honesty and with graciousness. I would practice telling stories that encourage or inspire.

I would allow time for meaning to develop in unhurried conversations. I would maintain good eye contact when talking and actively listen to others. I would spend time reflecting on what is true, what is good, and what is beautiful around me and plan opportunities to share about it with others. I might take someone out for breakfast or for coffee just to chat. I would focus most of my attention as best I can on opportunities for genuine communication and make time in my schedule for the needs of others. I would do all these things first with my wife!

There are so many ways to create meaningful moments for ourselves and others. Let me end this section with another story from Dr. Steven Arrowsmith. I only found out about this some years after I got to know him. The story itself may not be an ideal illustration of how meaning is created, but the conditions in which I heard it created abundant meaning for me.

> Several hours into the mayhem of being separated at gunpoint from my wife and children, wondering if they were alive, being raped, or who knows what, of watching these guys ardently trying to steal everything (little as it was) we owned, of being tied to a chair, beat up a bit, and asked to talk about my spiritual beliefs as an AK-47 barrel was placed against the tip of my nose, after all of this it seemed irrational to continue in any hope. But then it began to get worse. We had been temporarily living in someone else's nice home and had assiduously stayed away from the personal belongings of the owner. Unbeknownst to me, one thing we had not explored was a cabinet that turned out to contain some nice Scotch. But the bad dudes found it. Things had seemed bleak, but the reality of eight well-armed paratroopers in my home crossed into new territory when they began to get drunk. Now the only rational conclusion I could reach was that this was to be the night of our deaths. All of us.

In the moment that reality struck home, that there were no options, there was nothing I could do to change anything about what was happening and going to happen, no way for me to protect my wife and three young daughters, I experienced something I still cannot rationally explain. There was an immense sensation of quiet. Not the absence of sound, but a powerful invasion of calm. All the chaos going on in the house ceased to be relevant in the face of being transported into something else. Then, even crazier was the sudden awareness that someone was behind me. Though, since I was tied to my chair, I could not turn to confirm it, I suddenly knew that God the Father was physically, actually sitting back there, just out of sight and touch. Not as some vaguely assuring and ethereal presence, but He (the one with the capital H) had shown up. Or not shown up, but rather that He pulled back a curtain in some way for me to perceive what actually was and always had been going on.

It was as if I was given, temporarily and incompletely, a guest pass into a different room, right there, but completely different from where I was bound up. I was seeing the unseen, some new and larger dimension. It was obvious (don't ask me how), however, that He was not there to do what I wanted and had fervently prayed. All I wanted was to be out of this beastly situation. He was not only reminding me, but also allowing me to physically experience, that He was there to be with me through all of this. No matter how this all played out, including the very likely possibility of dying in the next few minutes, He wasn't going anywhere. I wasn't alone. I wasn't going to die alone. And if I died, there was something, somewhere else, very nearby, ready to welcome me. As it turned out, we didn't die, but some of my old ways of thinking did.

THE IMPORTANCE OF BEING HUMAN

I heard this story sitting with Steve in the lounge of an airport somewhere in Europe waiting for our international flight to somewhere in Africa. I was profoundly affected by the deep meaning of the moment as he told this story. Over the years, it has provided a sort of touchstone for me when challenges seemed overwhelming. I have been more aware of the presence of the Creator ever since.

How to act as an agent of restoration

One of my eye surgeon trainees was a bright and enthusiastic African surgeon from Togo. He had been through two training programs but still lacked some of the skills he needed to achieve good results. I did not realize it at the time, but he came to me as a sort of "trainer of last resort." The training I offered was free of charge, and the director of his training program, frustrated with his lack of progress, wanted a way to get him to move on. I noticed he had some surgical habits that were causing complications and started working to address these problems. He made some progress, but then things significantly changed one Friday morning during a gathering of patients for their final postoperative check.

The patients gathered as a group every Friday for what we called "Celebrate Sight Day." I had designed this as a chance for the patients to express how they felt about the service they had received and how it impacted their lives. It was encouraging to the whole team, but I insisted that all trainees attend as part of their training. These events communicated the value of their work better than anything I could ever say.

On this particular Friday, I noticed my trainee with a huge smile on his face and tears in his eyes watching the patients dancing and singing at the top of their lungs. He was a large man, and I walked over to stand next to him, hoping to get some idea of what was going through his mind. He leaned down and said, "Now I know why I am here. I am here to give sight to my people!" He could see himself in the picture for the first time. He went on to become one of the best surgeons I ever trained, starting a training program in his own country to share what had been given to him. He even launched his own foundation to serve those who could not afford eye surgery. This surgeon became an agent of change and hope because hope changed him.

The essential attitudes of change agents

To be an agent of change, you must have hope that change is possible and that you are designed to participate in producing that change. Now that you have studied your design and started developing skills to live by your design, let me suggest a few attitudes that will help you become an agent of change. You could call these "The Essential Attitudes for Change Agents" if you wanted a title for it.

First, you must have the attitude that life is a combined spiritual and material faith walk, not a mechanistic or fatalistic exercise in futility. Remember that choosing faith over fatalism is not some mind game, nor is it positive thinking or religious conviction(see Chapter 10). Faith is the essential link to hope because it helps me see that I, as a human being, fit perfectly into the cosmic order

THE IMPORTANCE OF BEING HUMAN

around me. It's my connection with an invisible order existing in the visible realm. It's what allows me to find wholeness as a spiritual being in a visible world that I do not control but one in which my Creator is present.

Second, you must have the attitude that your engagement with life really matters. This attitude leads to daily choices to participate in life rather than death, good rather than evil, and beauty rather than ugliness. This attitude encourages us to use Wisdom and discernment to find the best opportunities to live, not just survive. It moves us towards experiences of love and meaning in committed but flawed relationships where there is real risk and real cost.

Third, you must have an attitude of hopefulness in the reality of a new and good creative process at work in you and in our world. In other words, you must have an attitude of optimism about the possibility of positive change no matter how difficult. You must avoid the attitude of despair that humanity is spiraling down the tube to annihilation. You don't need to pretend that all is well—it clearly is not—but you must maintain an attitude of confidence that even in the messiness of life, there is more at play than what you can see. You need this confidence to participate in and celebrate the restoration that is occurring.

I have no doubt that the world is deteriorating in many ways, often caused by the same human beings who are supposed to be creating love and significance in it. Yet, as an agent of restoration, I find that I can often be part of the solution, not just for my own world, but for others as well—and so can you! But we must have faith that life is ordered not random, conviction that what we do matters, and hope that despite all the evil around us, there is a good

Creator at work to bring about restoration rather than annihilation.

Visualizing a "new" you

I hope all these ideas help you visualize new potential for your life as an agent of restoration. Of course, there is a lot more to it than just visualizing. Change never occurs in a vacuum. There are always others around you changing at the same time and in different ways. Conditions change. There is a cost to making changes. But these changes do begin with seeing new possibilities. The process can be painful, but out of this pain comes something incredible—a new creation is born! To us, this new creation appears like a miraculous birth because we cannot see the whole picture of the Creator's Spirit at work restoring creation, restoring relationships, and restoring hope.

It may help to visualize the path to being an agent of restoration like the picture shown.

I hope the direction is becoming clear. And I trust you are ready to get in the car to start the journey. But I still have to ask, "Why is the road so difficult? Why is it so hard to act like human beings if this is how we are designed to behave? Why is it such a long and bumpy road to change? Why did I need all this explanation and work if it all just comes naturally?" The reason, simply put, is that our ability comes naturally, but our choices do not. We have to choose the path we will take. This, of course, goes back to the same question: If our choices to live fully as human beings do not come naturally, how do we live by our divine design?

This leads to Part 3 in which we consider what role the Creator

THE IMPORTANCE OF BEING HUMAN

might have in our life as human beings. How can we choose to live by our divine design unless there is some connection with the Designer? The small steps of faith I suggested in Parts 1 and 2 now require another step of faith to consider what the Creator has revealed about all this. We must explore the resources the Creator has provided and how to access them. It's time to face the inevitable question of whether or not the Creator is actually and truly present in our world today.

What we have discussed in Part 1 and Part 2 is a powerful tool for personal growth. But I would invite you to take one more step with me into the unseen realm of the Creator's domain. I warn you that this could become uncomfortably personal, and quite spiritual sounding, but I assure you that it will be worth it. We must examine the realm of the Creator to have a sense of what the Creator has done in designing us.

The best way I know to explore this realm is through the eyes of Jesus, the Jewish rabbi who lived 2,000 years ago. I think you owe it to yourself to check it out. What if His story informs our story? Best I can tell from what Jesus' biographers have written, His whole purpose was to show us the importance of being human by giving us access to the unseen realm of the Creator, which He claimed had come to earth.

Take a minute to review this summary of Chapter 15 before you proceed. I think it will help you pull the picture together.

To help me reach my goal of creating love, I must practice attitudes and actions that enable me to:
- Trust that my divine design is built to produce love.
- Find opportunities to engage compassionately with others.
- Display truth, beauty, and goodness in everyday life.
- Practice sacrificial kindness.
- To help me reach my goal of creating opportunities for meaningfulness, I must practice attitudes and actions that enable me to:
- Trust that my divine design is built to produce meaning.
- Be all-in about the "small things" of life.
- Connect life experiences with the bigger story of creation.
- Practice making waves that disrupt the mundane

patterns of life.
- To effectively and consistently use the essentials of my divine design as an agent of change, I must consider:
- The reality of a future determined by faith, not by circumstances, personal strengths, or fate.
- Full engagement in wisely chosen restorative and creative opportunities.
- The ongoing cost of doing life in a way that produces light for restoring and sustaining my primary functions (authority, dignity, and virtue) and energy for creating love and meaning.
- The hope of a new creation process at work in me and in my world.

The proper functioning of my whole operational design, not personal perfection, enables me to move forward in the hope of being fully human and having an impact in my world.

Glenn Strauss, M.D.

Part 3

Remembering the story of the Creator

Glenn Strauss, M.D.

Chapter 18

Our built-in capacity for faith

I hope you've continued reading because you want to take a serious look at the unseen realm of the Creator's domain. I am absolutely convinced that a step into this domain is necessary to get the full benefit of your divine design. We have studied the tragic story of humanity (Part 1) and discussed how to tell a new story using our divine design (Part 2). Now I must tell the story of the Creator to bring it all together.

I know for many it's a stretch to explore "spiritual" concepts, especially if it involves discussing Jesus. After all, we live in a postmodern culture that tells us that "truth" does not exist outside of our own experience. The fact that Jesus claims to reveal cosmic and universal truths certainly does not fit with our paradigm. I am aware that Jesus is often seen as a character fabricated to manipulate the masses for a religious agenda. From this point of view, Jesus is, at best, a myth or a legend.

But what if Jesus is much more than that? What if Jesus really is the Designer who lived among us as a human being? I think we can use the story of Jesus to explain human existence from the Designer's point of view. I am not trying to prove anything other than what is already self-evident: Human beings really do exist. And since we exist, there must be an observable design for optimal function. And if there is a design, there must be a Designer. If Jesus is that Designer, the implications of His participation in our story are just too significant to overlook as we explore the importance of being human.

I understand this may already sound too religious for some, but hear me out on this before drawing any conclusions. What follows are not Sunday school answers, religious jargon, or evangelical Bible thumping. I admit that I am a product of such things, but I have gotten over most of that to discover what is at the heart of it all. I don't want you to end up missing the most important thing about life as a human being: We are able to engage with our Creator right here and right now to bring love and meaning into our world. This is possible because Jesus provides an open door into His spiritual domain, right here and right now. This is an astonishing, magnificent, and life-changing reality. And if it's really true—and I'm convinced it is—it changes everything.

You needed a bit of faith to accept my observations and reasoning in Parts 1 and 2. Now you will need to lean on faith as a primary tool! This is a critical point because I will use the 2,000-year-old story of Jesus to tell the Creator's story. Faith is needed because the story of Jesus lacks physical evidence and offers no tangible proof of exactly what transpired in His lifetime. But if you will give me a chance, I hope to dispel skepticism by showing how His story and ours actually complete and reinforce each other. (See Appendix 1 for more detail.) You simply can't have one without the other—they are mutually validating. Since our existence is indisputable, the Creator's is too! No wonder the story of Jesus is so compelling (though often doubted) even today. As we dive into His story, I hope you will see that it validates and expands on much of what we have been discussing. Let me summarize it for you here.

The story of Jesus provides context for the understanding of our own story: God always existed; God creates a cosmos; God creates humanity, which rebels against Him; God executes a plan to rescue humanity and restore creation by becoming a human being He names Jesus (literally "the Rescuer").

On the other hand, our story completes the Creator's story: Mankind, uniquely bearing the image of the Creator, is given the role of ruling creation with the Creator; mankind forfeits its right to bear that image by rebelling; mankind designs and repeatedly executes self-defeating and destructive plans to maintain control of its own image; a new man (Jesus) restores mankind's right to bear the image of God so that we can again work in partnership with the Creator to restore the good creation. The story of Jesus brings together the story of the Creator and the story of mankind with clarity and consistency.

Before we can really get into a discussion about the story of Jesus, I would like to say a little more about faith. In our cultural context, faith is a confusing concept. We've discussed in detail that faith is not the same thing as positive thinking (see Chapter 10). So what is it? Jesus is quoted as frequently saying that we should embrace "the faith of a child." Perhaps He wanted His audience to embrace a fundamental part of their design, a part that had been long hidden by religion and self-deception but urgently needed to be revived. What if faith is as important as breathing?

Glenn Strauss, M.D.

Faith is the secret sauce

Jesus did not think children were perfect—He just noticed how their reality was set in the moment. Just think about how embarrassingly honest a four-year-old can be in public. What is real to children is the story they are living, not the facts and complexity of the world. They don't try to figure out what is true in any larger sense. They live, as Jesus observed, by faith—not a "religious" faith, but a practical faith in what they imagine is going on around them.

As adults, we like to think we are a bit more sophisticated. We like to believe that facts shape our choices and that well-reasoned arguments determine our beliefs. The truth is, they do not. Think about how often adults rationalize and justify behaviors, lying to themselves and others. Adults say things like, "That's my story, and I'm sticking to it," even if the story makes no sense. People like to tell what my wife and I call "stupid lies"—irrational stories constructed to justify bad choices. The stories we believe determine the choices we make, regardless of the facts.

It seems obvious that we regularly make choices without knowing all the facts. Sometimes, it's the best we can do. We choose which product to purchase, which doctor to consult, which movie to see, whom to marry, etcetera, etcetera, all without absolute certainty. How do we do it? My observation is that there is something within each one of us—the same "faith of a child" that Jesus observed—that enables us to process uncertainty and make a choice.

Most animals react instinctively. They don't analyze if the

threat they perceive is real or not. We, on the other hand, are designed as rational and spiritual beings to react by choice. Faith (and I do not mean religious faith) is an integral part of our operational design that enables us to make choices rather than be paralyzed by fear of the unknown. Despite our limitations, we survive and thrive by choosing between alternatives rather than instinctive reactions. We do have instincts, but these need not control us. We are designed with the unique human ability to filter out uncertainty about what we don't know so we can act on what we do know.

Let me just say for the record that the idea of faith was not invented by Christians. We in the developed world have made "faith" a religious thing. As a result, matters of "faith" have proliferated into religious dogmas that have divided humanity and indeed the followers of Jesus as well, for thousands of years. Wars have been fought, families divided, factions and denominations formed, tribes eliminated, and political systems built, all to defend what are usually only preferences and personal agendas. Faith has been distorted to suit our needs. Instead of being a gift tucked away in our design that has the potential to unite, empower, and align us with the Creator, faith has become a curse. Faith has, in effect, been weaponized by modern Christianity. My evangelical friends will not be too happy to hear it said this way, but it's all too true.

We have made faith a competition, piling up competing evidence to see whose stack is bigger. By making faith a competition, we draw the battle lines between truth and lies, between science and religion, between right and wrong, between the physical and the spiritual. This is a no win-win solution—only

Glenn Strauss, M.D.

lose-lose.

I think we are missing the point of faith entirely. In the end, faith is not about proof; it is about preference. The faith of a child, the faith that is built into our design, is the ability to choose what we prefer and act on it—and in general, you choose the story that is enjoyable, meaningful, and special to you. There is no absolute "proof" on either side of the faith vs. science debate. Both claim their proof is absolute—but in reality, it is not. (Please note that I do acknowledge the existence of absolute truth. I am only pointing out the fallacy of rhetorical proof for that truth.) I would define "faith" as the critical part of our divine design enabling us to make a choice based on a preference in matters with no absolute conclusion. It's the secret sauce that makes our design work in a complex world that would otherwise overwhelm and paralyze us with fear of the unknown. Faith is essential for building trust when there are no absolutes.

One last point about faith. Since it's embedded in our design, expressing faith is as inescapable as hunger. As part of our spiritual nature, we inevitably use faith as a tool to choose what to believe, what we "prefer," even in our scientifically and technologically advanced world. To say it another way, you cannot help but put your faith in something because there is never enough absolute proof to give you absolute certainty about anything. But there is no reason to despair: Truth is out there, safely held in the hands of the Designer and Creator of all things and often revealed to us as Wisdom. Without Truth, there would be total chaos. Without Wisdom, there would be total despair. Without faith, there would be paralyzing fear—human beings could never have the Wisdom to enjoy and thrive in the order that Truth brings to creation. The Creator has embedded within our divine design the capacity to live by faith. All we need is the right story to ignite it.

What's the story here?

I was stunned by how important stories are to people living in less "developed" nations. As I traveled and immersed myself in other cultures less "advanced" than my own, I came to understand that storytelling was a way of understanding life. I, of course, come from a culture where facts are what really matter. So, I explained what I thought were helpful "facts" about everything from hygiene to creation. They sometimes found my facts interesting—but they rarely found them to be very significant.

I finally realized that they just wanted to know my story. This is what they needed to trust me to guide them. If I explained the facts of handwashing, they politely listened. If I told my personal experience with someone dying because they didn't wash their hands, that got their attention. The facts just made more sense in the context of a story.

Over the years I have learned the most important question I can ask when faced with uncertainty is, "What's the story here?" I have learned that this question is a way to turn on my built-in faith. It's the question that helps me remember that I cannot know it all, that there is a story much bigger than me, and that (consciously or unconsciously) we all want stories that give us security and success. At a superficial level, it may be as simple as seeing yourself as an effective speaker, confidently standing up to make a presentation.

But at a deeper level, there may be the nagging questions about your existence. What's the story here? How do you prefer to see yourself—accident of nature or the result of a design? Do you prefer seeing yourself as a sentient, physical and spiritual being created in the image of a loving Designer as I have explained, or instead as something more like a sophisticated machine, a sophisticated biological process, or even a blob of well-evolved goo; or, for the sci-fi lovers among us, as a being designed by aliens and left on Earth to be watched and toyed with as an experiment?

I am writing because you owe it to yourself to consider the stories of Jesus. In the end, your faith will kick in and deal with the uncertainties in the story I am telling. Some may hide their faith under piles of scientific "facts" or stories like the myths we discussed in Part 1. Others may dilute their faith with modern religious practices and self-deception. But just remember that those who were introduced to Jesus 2,000 years ago made a dangerous, life-changing choice. Many of them never actually saw Jesus, but they heard the reports of the eyewitnesses. They recognized that His story was something new and unbiased by the long history of human and religious failure. With the faith of a child, they eagerly chose to give their lives for it. This is how the life and message of Jesus ignited a movement that changed the world.

I cannot help but think there is another dramatic shift coming. Tired religious institutions and the obsession with self that have obscured the story of Jesus for hundreds of years will be overwhelmed by a tsunami of people already advancing undetected as a small disturbance in the ocean. As it nears the shores of our institutions, it will become an enormous wave that wipes out what

THE IMPORTANCE OF BEING HUMAN

we have built so it can be replaced by people whose lives tell the story of humanity's partnership with our Creator. It may not be in my lifetime, but maybe my grandchildren or their children will see it happen.

One of the New Testament authors describes the challenge of faith for those who would continue the mission of the resurrected Jesus: "Let us run with endurance the race designed for us as human beings, looking to Jesus, the originator and perfecter of a faith that is focused on the joy of seeing the Creator's plan unfold. Though He endured pain and shame leading to death on a Roman cross, this same Jesus, now resurrected, sits in the place of honor, in an as yet unseen realm on earth, surrounded by all those who throughout their lives witnessed His triumph over evil to bring us His heavenly domain" (Hebrews 12:1–2, my paraphrase).

In Part 2, I discussed visualizing the life for which we are designed as human beings. In Part 3, I want to help you visualize and engage with the stunning possibility of life enhanced and completed by a spiritual existence. I hope to provide a suitable starting point for you to explore the prospect of human life by faith in a divine framework. I have divided the fundamental concepts we will explore into three sections:

1. What the Creator has revealed in the story of Jesus about being human.
2. What it means to receive the spiritual enhancements offered by the Creator for augmenting our basic operational design.
3. How to use our operational design and its enhancements so we can live in partnership with our

Creator.

I hope this sparks your imagination and encourages you to read on. We begin in Chapter 19 with the idea that the Creator has revealed critical information about a divine framework for human existence in the story of Jesus. This Jewish messianic figure who lived over 2,000 years ago clearly moved the plot forward in the story of mankind. Much of how we view our world today can be traced back to this one time in history. It seems reasonable to ask what His story might reveal about being human, what it reveals about the importance of being human, and where this might take us in the future.

Chapter 19

Exploring what the Creator reveals about being human

If the Creator were going to show up in creation, it seems to me this would have happened in a much more spectacular way than as a baby boy. Why not an apocalyptic alien visitation, an angelic invasion, or a heavenly army in the sky raining down terror on humanity because of all our failures? It turns out that the human revelation of the Creator was "apocalyptic," but only in the literal sense (i.e., a stunning revelation of something entirely new), not the "end of the world" sense. Jesus was the launching point of a new creation project. His story has much to tell us about ourselves and our place in this project and where it is headed. We can find hope in the story of Jesus.

To begin with, the birth story of Jesus certifies that our design is exactly what the Creator envisioned for humanity. When Jesus' birth was announced as the Son of God AND the son of man, it was the Creator's seal of approval and a proclamation of peace between the Creator and man. Otherwise, why would the Creator be born as a man? Why tell the story this way? Why not reveal a new creature never before seen? Imagine if the Creator decided that the old model of humanity was out of date and came up with a new and improved, sexually neutral Dr. Suess figure! Apparently, the Creator did not think we lost our relevance in creation.

By the way, please understand, this has nothing to do with Jesus being a male; the point is, Jesus came as a human being because there was no mistake in our operational design. We are all made with body, mind, and spirit, limitations and all, exactly the way we are intended—both men and women. Humanity is the work of art that the Creator wanted to use as the one image that best reflects all aspects of His divine character and nature in the physical realm. It takes both men and women to fully rise to this honor and privilege.

Second, when Jesus was born human as the "Son of God," it restored something to humanity that was lost for centuries. To get the full picture, I must take us back to the Creator's story as it was revealed by Jesus starting with where we enter the picture.

From the start, the Creator designed us with the right as human beings to rule the newly created physical space as His partners or co-regents. Think of it: According to this story, we were uniquely designed to have dominion over creation as an extension of the Creator. This birthright was tragically forfeited because of the rebellion of humanity soon after creation. In the process, we also lost access to our birthplace, "the Garden of Eden," as it is called in the story (literally the fruitful or pleasurable garden of God). We could never go "home." We were forced out of the one place perfect for us in the newly planted and expanding world, and consequently, lost the job for which we were perfectly designed, all because we wanted something more. It seemed our potential would be forfeited unless a suitable human was born to restore the birthright to the family of mankind. Every bit of evidence about the life of Jesus suggests He is that person, conceived as a human being so the unfulfilled potential for humanity could be restored through a new bloodline.

But Jesus had no physical children with which to pass on the birthright (despite what some modern authors and movies suggest). Instead, our birthright is passed on by a resource hidden in our fundamental human design—our capacity for faith as spiritual beings. In Chapter 11, we discussed the possibility that a small seed of faith in our divine design will ignite hope, which fuels our "fusion engine" to create love and meaning. We took this one step further in Chapter 16 to say that faith is wired into our human design and essential for living life in a complex world. Now I am suggesting that faith finds its ultimate fulfillment when used to bring us back to the story of our birthright as human beings.

In a way, faith offers human beings access to a literal "new birth" (as Jesus fittingly refers to this spiritual transaction) into a different family line equipped once again to fulfill its birthright. Jesus' coming as a human baby was exactly what was needed for humanity to reclaim its birthright as partners with the Creator. Jesus started a new family in which human beings, by faith, become His legal brothers and sisters.

Third, the human birth of Jesus forever links the created with the Creator in an intimate and personal way. Jesus, the Son of God, the Creator of the cosmos, is born the Son of Man (as He is often called in the Bible), and by doing so, has chosen to forever remain human. The Creator has elected to become part of His creation, not just a visitor to it like some distant deity waiting for us to get our lives straightened out before occasionally gracing us with His presence. The Creator now and will always share the experience of our human limitations. The story of humanity and the story of the Creator are inseparable. This cannot be undone by the force of time or effort or even by God Himself.

Did you ever wonder why the Creator did not just start over again if we really messed up creation that badly? I believe it is because the Creator can only create, not uncreate. A "Creator" (who by definition is purely creative) can only bring things into existence out of some impulse to add, complete, or enhance. I think we could use the word "love" to describe this essential impulse for creation. There is no impulse towards destruction. The creative impulse is revealed dramatically in the story of Jesus, the Creator, recreating Himself as a human being. Rather than annihilating humanity for our failures, the Creator, in a stunning act of love, is born as a human being to connect His story with ours. He was born physically to reconnect us with our place in creation once and for all.

But that's not all!

What a life . . . and death . . . and Life!

Jesus grew up in a complex world along far Eastern and African trade routes in a Jewish community under Roman rule and Greek philosophical influence. At first, His life was nothing spectacular (unless you believe the story of Him turning clay models into live birds as it says in the Qur'an). But without a doubt, those last three years were quite incredible. The story unfolds as a seemingly ordinary man reveals a hidden spiritual domain come to earth. It's a story of hope in the context of political misrepresentation, a philosophical misunderstanding of pain, a religious misinterpretation of life, and an economic structure producing massive poverty. He perseveres through personal discouragement and betrayal only to end up dying a horrible and unjust death. Jesus introduced a simple countercultural message of hope into His complex world and paid the price for it.

As many people know, the story takes a major turn when Jesus returns as a resurrected human being following His death and burial. His stunned followers see Him experiencing life in a new and incredible way—full of joy, royal authority, and regal honor, physically appearing and disappearing, even walking through walls but still enjoying fresh fish. The early followers of Jesus saw a new creation process at work, evidenced by the resurrected Jesus as a new type of human being with access to both the existing physical realm and a new spiritual realm on earth.

The return of Jesus as an immortal human being was the solid evidence that a new type of life was possible and available to anyone. The story of the resurrection of the Creator made it clear that the pain of meaningless death was over and the battle for rule of the heavenly domain on earth was won.

A new chapter has begun

I find it remarkable that Jesus removed himself physically from the world before it was clear that any of His work mattered. Only one author (Luke) cryptically describes Jesus "parting" from the disciples as He is giving them a final blessing. Where did He go and why? I really don't think His followers knew for sure. All they knew was that within six short weeks after His resurrection, Jesus was gone and took with Him a resurrected body that could have spearheaded the movement He started. Little did they know that His apparent "disappearing act" was a move that would seal His loving partnership with humanity forever. It was actually the beginning of a new chapter in our story.

Here's how it played out according to historical accounts. After His death, apparent resurrection, and subsequent disappearance, Jesus gives His followers time to assemble in Jerusalem and think about all that had occurred. Scared and disorganized, they huddle to discuss the events. They eat, they pray . . . a lot! About forty days later (which probably seemed like forever to them), Jesus returns to them, but not as a man. He returns to the physical realm of His followers as a Spirit. And not just any spirit. This was the Spirit of God Himself—the One who came to be called the Holy Spirit. The Spirit spoken of in the Torah who hovered over creation, shaping and perfecting it from the beginning of time. The Spirit who brought order. The Spirit who entered the first man and woman as the very breath of the Creator, giving them physical and spiritual life.

These early followers came to find out that Jesus had victoriously taken His seat as the King of a new spiritual Kingdom. Not only that, they also discover that the Spirit of Jesus Himself was still present in their world just as He had promised! They discovered that the human Jesus was physically positioned in the new earthly spiritual domain so that He could operate freely by His

Spirit in the physical realm. And as a Spirit, He could move among all His followers everywhere in the world, all at once, to finish the work He started. New life was given, a new Kingdom was born, and a new chapter in the story of humanity began!

It's way bigger than any church

Jesus promised His first followers that He had come to stay, and so He did! For us this means He is still here, not off in some distant heaven. The incredible events after the death and resurrection of Jesus prove that the Creator is all-in to restore and dwell in His creation along with humanity. And all this is because of His divine love, not some angry response to how we have messed up His world. He likes it here and plans to stay around in the world for a long time—actually forever. And He is at work right now to set things right!

As a result of these events, the domain of Jesus extends over all creation. No one can claim an exclusive right to God's presence; the Creator is not bound to any one nation, church, or people. I love how the Apostle Paul says it in one of his poems: "He is before all things and in Him all things have their existence" (Colossians 1:17). He even quotes two Greek poets of his day (Epimenides and Aratus), who sing of a Creator "who is not far from any of us in whom we live and move and have our being" (Acts 17:27–28). The Creator expresses himself wherever and whenever He chooses. When those who follow Him gather with two or three or with thirty-thousand others, it's because they believe Jesus is there expressing His presence from His spiritual realm by His Spirit. Believers gather to celebrate a domain without walls (at least that's what they should be doing). It's so much bigger than any one church, and it is so much closer than we think—only a step of faith away.

Something even better is coming

We will have something even greater to celebrate in the future. Jesus taught His followers that one day His spiritual realm would be fully integrated with the whole of the physical realm. He was clear that He would again be physically present as the two realms join through a series of final, indescribable events. Who knows when that will be or what exactly it will look like—not even Jesus knows. In what will be the final chapter of the story, the Creator will be fully present, evil will fade into nothingness (not just sequestered off somewhere), and we will be fully human, exercising authority over the whole of an ongoing new creation.

Those who want no part of the Creator's story won't be; they'll have no part in it in any way. It will be as if they simply never existed. (In the Bible, the image is that of being thrown out on the pile of refuse in the Valley of Hinnom outside Jerusalem—literally Gehenna or "hell"—to be burned until there is nothing left.) But those who want to be part of the Creator's story will be, living as immortal beings surrounded by the goodness of the Creator and His creation as it continues to grow and develop. (And just as a little brainteaser for those who appreciate a good story, think about the fact that we could be part of another story yet to be told!) Whatever eternity holds in store for us, I am certain it's not sitting around, plucking a harp on a cloud somewhere in blissful laziness while others suffer in evil agony. Evil will no longer exist. Only the glory of God will remain, filling everything everywhere!

It's all about love

This still doesn't explain why the Creator would do such a crazy thing like becoming human. One of the most quoted Bible verses says, "For God so loved the world that He gave His only begotten Son, so that whoever believes in Him should not perish but have eternal life" (John 3:16). Perhaps the answer is as simple as that. It seems clear that the Creator is driven by love for us—the same impulse that resulted in the creation of the cosmos. If Jesus is known for anything, it's for His love. No matter what else you may think about Him, you must admit, Jesus did do love right. And He claimed that the love He demonstrated was the love of the Creator.

Let me point out here that human beings are not some kind of favorite toy. The love Jesus represented was far deeper than some whimsical fancy for human beings. Rather, Jesus expressed a deep and abiding love like that of a mother for a child, or a father for a son, or a friend willing to die for a friend. It was a love for creation that played out as a love story for humanity with Jesus making the ultimate sacrifice for us. The Creator went all-in for creation by going all-in for us.

The evidence is clear and overwhelming that the spiritual realm of Jesus is still on earth. It's filled with all those who are pouring life and love into it, literally re-creating what we have damaged and lost! How else do we explain the transformation of culture and millions of personal lives over the past 2,000 years by such a simple message given by a Jewish rabbi? How else can we explain so many visions of things happening in an unseen realm, near-death experiences providing glimpses into heaven, the miracles still occurring in Jesus' name, and the willingness of thousands to give their lives for this one man? The dark corruption in which humanity persists and our wretched attempts to institutionalize, politicize, and monetize the truth of the story of Jesus has not stopped the unstoppable Kingdom.

Faith, hope, and love

There is no way around it. You must decide the story in which you prefer to live. Even in the most difficult of conditions, it's still up to you to decide what the story is. It's faith that helps you make this choice. But let me ask you, how many times have you been disappointed by a story you believed that turned out to be untrue? Faith built on stories that fail us produces hope that disappoints us.

We've already talked a lot about the stories that will fail in Part 1. These are the modern myths of our culture. You can keep waiting for more evidence, more science, more proof, or more spiritual experiences. You could choose a story that revolves totally around you, some impersonal facts, religious organizations, or even some alien force. But you could just as easily embrace a partnership with the loving Creator in a new creation process occurring all around you even as you read this. Faith in the myths of our culture will fail. But faith in the story of a loving Creator—whose very image I bear—this faith will not fail.

Even a slight preference for the story of the Creator is enough to ignite the hope that fuels our divine design. This is a hope that does not disappoint because it's built on faith in the surety of a loving Creator. Jesus likens faith that can move mountains to a tiny mustard seed. He is not saying we should have faith in our ability to move mountains. He is saying that from small beginnings, faith can become a deeply rooted tree of conviction. And once that occurs, just hold on for the ride! Your divine operational design will start producing love and meaning far beyond all that you can ask or think. To use a Jesus metaphor—it will be like moving mountains!

In the next two chapters, we will discuss a few specific "changes" that will be needed to take this journey. I can see the frustration on your face already: Here it comes—he's just going to tell me this is all up to me. Well, actually, if you read on, you will see that the changes I am talking about are unique design enhancements that followers of Jesus are given to prepare you for this trip. In the end, for change to occur, we need time and resources, not determination.

Glenn Strauss, M.D.

Chapter 20

Receiving the spiritual enhancements offered by the Creator

I suppose you could say human beings are a sort of beautiful mess. We live in the middle of problems mostly of our own making, with a divine design that is supposed to be just what this world needs. We would like to believe that we are able to overflow with the love of the Creator, and yet we are so flawed. So, what is the secret for getting our human mojo going? Why is it so hard to act like human beings? Why do we need all this explanation and work if it's supposed to come "naturally"? The reason, simply put, is that our ability comes naturally—but our choices do not.

As I pointed out in the previous chapter, our choices tend to follow the story we believe regardless of the facts. If we do not believe the story of the Creator, our choices are unavoidably limited by a mortal existence and our own limitations—there's no frame of reference for anything more. It's true that faith in our divine design can produce amazing creativity and even sincere kindness. But if you add faith in the Creator's story to the mix, our range of potential choices expands dramatically. It takes you beyond the limitations of your mortal existence, and your choices will begin to show it. Over time, new patterns of behavior will most certainly develop. Remember: change the story, change the choices!

However (and this is a hugely significant "however"), new habits take time and resources to develop, and unfortunately, no matter which story you believe, this means living through lots of bad choices while growing into the potential of your new perspective. We could all use some assistance with navigating the way and curating our choices. The purpose of these final chapters is to explore the resources provided by the Creator when we choose a journey of faith. It turns out, these resources are found in a relationship with Jesus.

Who doesn't want a free upgrade

The same loving Designer who created, designed, and partners with us in our own story also gifts us with the enhancements we need to thrive as participants in His. And He does so freely! This expression of unmerited favor by the Creator is what the Bible refers to as grace. Grace takes us above and beyond bearing the Creator's image to being participants in His divine existence. Grace takes us out of the corrupt domain of our own world and transports us into the restorative spiritual domain of the Creator.

For the early followers of Jesus, it was as if all of life suddenly become a joyful, albeit disorienting, invitation to a new world. They gradually worked out what was happening and recorded what they considered to be their most important memories for future generations. The New Testament gives us a window into their thoughts, their struggles, and their attempts to guide and instruct others, even as the "Helper" whom Jesus promised was guiding and instructing them.

A careful look at their writings suggests there were at least three unique ways Jesus supported their growth after He was gone: They believed He shared His Life, His Kingdom, and His Spirit with them. They eagerly embraced these rather spectacular, gracious gifts as complete novices in spiritual living. They did not go to church as we know it. They did not go to a school for religious studies. They did not isolate themselves from the damaged world. They used the story they were told and these lavish gifts they were given to start living life in a new way. It was the perfect upgrade to the perfect human design that prepared them to be a blessing to the world.

I will use the rest of this chapter to familiarize you with these gifts.

Jesus shares His Life with us

The foundational gift received by the followers of Jesus was what He called the gift of "Life." This must have been a bit strange for them to hear considering they were all, in fact, alive. Stranger still is that Jesus tells them to expect that their lives would be more difficult, not less, even facing death if they chose to follow Him. Clearly, Jesus was not offering a "life" full of fun and easy living. Nor was He talking about giving them some kind of happy pill so they could just enjoy the difficulties. They came to understand that the Life Jesus spoke of could only arise from their death (metaphorically speaking of course), like a seed that is buried before it springs to life. The reason was simple: the Life Jesus was sharing could only be found in Him; it was not something that they would receive from Him. Jesus invites us to come to Him for Life.

To appreciate this incredible gift, let's go back to what we discussed about our divine operational design. It's important here to remember the key point—our design is a reflection of the Creator. We bear His image in our design. We are what we are as human beings because the Creator poured Himself into us. Just think of it: the fact that hope fueled by nothing more than faith supernaturally ignites an engine capable of producing life-giving energy; the fact that this energy generates love and meaning in life; the fact that we are able to function with authority, dignity, and virtue in such a messed up world, not to mention the fact that we have the ability to even imagine all this and embrace it without absolute proof. Is this particular combination of traits just extraordinarily good luck? I think not! Then why are we designed the way we are? It's because we are uniquely designed to share the Life of the loving Creator, who by nature possesses all these characteristics. We not only bear His image in our design—we also have the potential to share in His nature by faith.

But remember how daily life tends to fragment our lives? We discussed in Chapter 8 how our pursuit of success can lead to chaos and emptiness rather than life. The fact is, the way we choose to live can be the main barrier to realizing our potential for "Life." I think the early followers of Jesus realized that their faith was, in a sense, putting their lives together in a way that their own religious systems, cultures, philosophies, and political systems could not.

THE IMPORTANCE OF BEING HUMAN

With a spiritual awareness unlike anything they had ever experienced before, they found themselves experiencing the life of Jesus, sharing the same journey as He did, experiencing both His suffering and His resurrection Life.

Of course, most of us would prefer to share only in the resurrection part—but unfortunately that's not how it works. When we share a life with someone, we share the whole life, not just the good parts! The authority, dignity, and virtue we are designed to express as human beings when functioning at our best (discussed in Part 2) was modeled by Jesus—but so was sacrificial service. Faith, in some mysterious way, enables us to enter the fullness of Life in Jesus. No wonder Jesus said that He came so that we could have Life and have it abundantly (John 10:10)!

Jesus shares His Kingdom with us

Jesus not only shares His Life with us; He shares His Kingdom as well. He proclaimed repeatedly that His Kingdom was near and that His followers would see it emerge in their lifetime. In the end, He alone paid the ultimate price so that His Kingdom could rise triumphant. We were no help at all. But despite our uselessness then, Jesus freely shares all the resources of His Kingdom with us now.

The implications are profound. Full access to the Kingdom gives us two incredible privileges. First of all, it means that the authority of the King is personally available to us. Those of us with a faith connection to Jesus are actually seated with Him right now in a place of honor in this spiritual realm on earth. Maybe you haven't heard it this way before, but I assure you, it's all true. Check out the Apostle Paul's take on it in Ephesians 2:1-10.

It should be said that the early followers of Jesus were expecting Jesus to lead a political revolt that would rebuild Israel as an earthly Kingdom, free from slavery to Rome. What they got was the authority to rebuild the world as an extension of a heavenly Kingdom, launched by Jesus to free humanity from bondage to its ancient curse. In some supernatural way, heaven had come to set them free! They saw the authority of Jesus exhibited in nature, they saw it in each other, and they saw it in the inexplicable transformative effect of His words.

In time, those early followers came to appreciate what a privilege it was to possess the authority of this Kingdom. They understood that the phrase "in Jesus' name" was far more than the proper ending to a prayer. It was a statement of faith and courage to do what Jesus would do with His authority fully behind it. They were spreading the good news of Jesus as if they were Jesus himself. And by the way, this realization had nothing to do with studying the Bible as we know it today (there was no Bible). They immersed themselves in the life and teachings of Jesus as they lived out the story of the Creator's domain on earth. They did not just bear the image of God—they wore the likeness of Jesus in their lives! I would encourage you to read my companion book, *The Importance of Embracing Jesus,* to explore this more fully.

Full access to the Kingdom also offered a second even more astonishing privilege: We are allowed and, in fact, invited to come before the King anytime and anywhere. We who did nothing but believe a story have personal access to the Creator who told the story. Early on in His teachings, Jesus encouraged His followers to approach the Creator directly as a dear heavenly Father. But this was wildly sacrilegious in their day. They only gradually came to understand that they could speak boldly and plainly with the Creator. Filled with wonder and gratitude and a bit of healthy fear, they found they could experience Him, know Him, and even enjoy Him. It was the greatest treasure of all.

The Life and Kingdom Jesus shares with us means that, even today, we are not just invited but also encouraged and equipped to continue the work He started. And our divine design is exactly the right framework with which to do it. But there is still one more gift to describe.

Jesus shares His Spirit with us

Perhaps the most surprising gift of all was that Jesus shared His own Spirit with His followers. All human beings have the same basic design including body, mind, and spirit. Jesus had this design, too, and this is His "Spirit" we are talking about here. How can one human being share his spirit with another human being? Crazy, right? Well, not in this case because this Spirit existed long before there was human life. This Spirit is a distinct component of an eternal Creator. And as a unique but coexistent eternal entity, this Spirit is fully shareable! That's a mouthful, but let me explain.

The Bible contains a record of some of our oldest oral traditions passed down from the beginning of our story. According to this record, the Holy Spirit was present at creation and gave Life to the first human being. But after the first man and woman were expelled from their garden oasis, this Spirit could no longer live with mankind. Instead, He periodically showed up in the lives of prophets, priests, kings, and others to accomplish specific tasks. During the journey of Israel to the Promised Land, this same Spirit lived in a holy tabernacle (ornate tent), appearing as a pillar of fire at night and a cloud by day to literally lead them out of Egyptian captivity. There are many other examples of the Spirit's activities, all of which fit Jesus' simple description of the Holy Spirit as a part of God who is "like the wind"—a moving, powerful force only God himself could direct, like the story of Jesus calming the "wind."

This force is exactly what the early followers of Jesus experienced as the Holy Spirit came to them during the Jewish feast of Pentecost, a celebration of the Torah, their national constitution. As if carried in by a huge windstorm, the Spirit came to rest on the disciples who were gathered for prayers. Reminiscent of the pillar of fire that led their people in the wilderness, they experienced the Presence of God as tongues of fire resting individually over each one's head as if to show that no tabernacle or temple was needed—only their individual lives. The Spirit then empowered them with all the languages needed to speak to the multinational crowds gathered for the festival. The Torah was now replaced by God himself speaking the words of truth. It was the beginning of a mission to the world.

As you might imagine, explaining this new Presence in each of their lives was a bit hard to describe objectively. A "mighty wind"? "Tongues of fire"? These were not mystics and philosophers. They were not experts in metaphysics or spiritualism. These were ordinary people aware of a new Presence within them. Over time, they described their perception of this Presence in many ways: as "seeing" Jesus dimly like in a mirror, as joy they could not explain, as "fruit" growing in their lives, as groaning that only God would understand, as remembrances of experiences with Jesus, as "callings" to serve and guidance about what to do, as inner peace they could not understand, and as desires rising up within them to forgive, to restore, and to heal. They experienced Jesus as the transformation of their own lives from within.

The Holy Spirit gave them a spiritual door to Jesus' Wisdom, His mind, His heart for others, His love, His peace, and His resurrection power. The Spirit allows us to totally immerse ourselves in the Life of Jesus. The Apostle Paul describes his life of faith in Jesus as if "Paul" no longer lived, but Jesus lived in him. For all the disciples, the years of trying to keep up with Jesus coming and going were now replaced by an abiding presence, accessible to each of them all the time.

But that was not all . . .

Jesus promised His followers that the Holy Spirit would be a "Helper," not just a Presence. As if the gift of His Presence were not enough, Jesus administered and coordinated unique, practical expressions of His Spirit in each of their lives! These "spiritual gifts," as they were called, were diverse and powerful tools for ministry covering a wide range of abilities, such as speaking, serving, teaching, and leading. Each gift enhanced and supplemented their human design. Each one helped the followers of Jesus carry out their mission mandate to expand the Kingdom to every tribe and nation on earth.

Today, I believe these gifts are still critical enhancements for our divine design and still fully available to all who follow Jesus. The shared Life Jesus offers, the Kingdom and authority He shares, and the Holy Spirit He gives are what make our design hum—body, mind, and Spirit working together to express the Designer's nature. Human beings are still impressive without these upgrades, but with them, we are unstoppable.

Visualize it like this:

It's true that in some Christian circles, these spiritual gifts sometimes become the focus. In others, these gifts are almost completely ignored. The Apostle Paul warns us all that love is the point, not these supernatural abilities; but however you see it, we ignore them at great cost to ourselves and the world around us. By keeping our eyes of faith on all that Jesus offers to share with us—"abiding in Him" as John, one Bible author puts it—we expand our human capacity to its full potential.

It takes a body

It might sound like I'm saying we don't need anyone else but Jesus. In a sense that's true. But we must understand that what Jesus shares with us individually to enhance our design, He gives to all His followers to unite us corporately. In fact, unity was the key message in His final address to His disciples before His death. Paul, the Apostle, describes how we should come together in unity like anatomical components to form the complete body of Jesus with Him as the head. The analogy is mind blowing: Since we each share in the Life of Jesus, we all share Life together as if we are His "body"—and it needs all of us to be complete. Each part has its own function operating in harmony with all the other parts. Coming together as a "body" leverages our individual design. When functioning properly, it acts as an amplifier of our energy for generating Life and delivering meaning to the world around it.

I realize I gave a rather harsh critique of religious institutions in Chapter 1. Churches today often do not function as they should—and I don't just mean that they are filled with imperfect people.

Sometimes church organizations are more concerned about protecting institutional integrity than about preserving human integrity. Sometimes they are modeled after modern business practices used to build successful volunteer organizations or family friendly entertainment centers. And I'm sorry to say, churches are even built to be modern PR agencies promoting political agendas, books, and egos. As sad as all that makes me, I am not suggesting we undermine or abandon these important elements of our social structure. But we must not be afraid to do whatever it takes to restore the true importance of being human even if this means looking outside of our religious institutions to find genuine spiritual community.

Personally, I think this means we need to think smaller and more locally rather than larger and more globally. Buildings and budgets are not requirements for effective community. Perhaps the opportunity for our best and most meaningful communities are close by with friends and neighbors. With a little effort, you might be able to find just what you need. Appendix 2 offers what I think are some helpful tips on how you might go about doing this.

In Chapter 5 we discussed how true individuality inspires the formation of healthy communities. We are quite capable of healthy social connections without any religious context. But just like the gifts that enhance our operational design, communities of faith are gifts that offer the protection, support, accountability, and encouragement we need to get the most out of our design and its enhancements. Faith communities should enable us to function with the fullness of our divine design, limitations and all. We would do well in our day to revisit the concept that Jesus' "body" is designed for love, not divisiveness, judgment, or political agendas.

Glenn Strauss, M.D.

Chapter 21

Learning to use your spiritual enhancements

We come to the point in our study where we must consider how to grow into our potential as human beings. Jesus has given us incredible resources, and we have an amazing design; wisdom is available to guide us—but now what? For starters, I've found that the task of being human begins by turning on your brain—and this usually means stepping away from the distractions we use to turn our brains off. Using and enjoying our incredible divine design and the divine gifts that enrich it begins with a series of mental tasks. Consider what we have discussed so far: We must first mentally embrace what it means to be human by applying Wisdom and rejecting the myths that hold our thinking captive (Part 1). Then, to act like human beings, we must mentally paint the picture of what it might look like if we were behaving according to our design (Part 2). Finally, we must do the mental task of exploring the new stories that help us embrace our potential as human beings (Chapters 16–18).

That is a lot of mental exercise, and these days, many people tend to be undisciplined, chaotic thinkers. In fact, we live in a culture that thrives on impulsivity ("just go for it"), not thoughtful reflection. In one sense, we are smarter than ever. But when it comes to deep thinking, we are asleep at the wheel, despite all the knowledge and study. We are lulled to sleep primarily by our conveniences—we rarely need to think deeply. Our brains are jarred awake only when our security and conveniences are threatened.

It's a challenge to find ways to turn on our brains. Modern life is often filled with repetitive, mind-numbing tasks and escapism, rather than simple activities that enlarge and expand our souls. Meaningful discussion and dialogue, literature, reflection, art, nature, music—all the experiences that inspire and expand our thinking—are handled more like special events than as part of our normal routines. For daily life we often choose to turn our brains off with parties, sports, video gaming, most entertainment, movies, and TV—all things that tend to bankrupt our thought life.

You may be surprised to hear that one of the most effective tools I have ever found for waking up my sleeping students is asking them unexpected questions. If I challenge someone with a good question, it tends to wake them up. They engage in active dialogue if they feel the question is worth answering. Trust me—it's not easy to come up with questions that students feel are worth answering. In fact, I spend more time developing questions than I do preparing presentations. The problem is that most of us ask questions to help us achieve something rather than to help us understand something. We tend to think of questions as problem-solving tools rather than as a discipline for interactively exploring the way we think about ourselves and the world.

Historically, the art of dialogue was taught as the primary system for learning thousands of years ago by the Greek philosopher Socrates. He observed that great truths came from great questions and taught his students how to use logic and synthesis interactively. The Socratic method, as it is called in learning theory today, is recognized as an effective tool for turning on the brain's higher functions, which include reasoning and judgment. The art of dialogue learning was only recently (in the 1990s) revived by the work of Dr. Jane Vella and others. Appendix 2 contains some useful tips I have developed to help you improve your skills in meaningful dialogue.

I'm not saying that life needs to be totally serious. Entertainment and distraction have a place in healthy living. I am saying that to have a meaningful life, you must make meaningful choices and this requires thoughtful living. We could all stand to be a little more intentional about mental activities that stimulate creativity and thinking. Remember that engaging in healthy dialogue is not about sounding smart; it's about being constructively curious—and anyone can be curious. Take time to reflect on what you have experienced and the conversations you've had. In the end, it's up to you keep your brain turned on. Without it, the potential of your design will remain untapped.

Get out of the chair

The next step in the process of integrating your spiritual enhancements into your life is taking action. We discussed at great length in Part 2 what it might look like if we are acting like human beings experiencing our divine design. It won't make any difference if you don't try a few of these ideas. Go out and find a community. Explore the world around you. Find new ways to be productive at your job. Volunteer for service. Go ahead and take a risk. Most good ideas die for lack of action.

I get how overwhelming it can be to actively try to change your behaviors. The inertia of old habits and the way of thinking that supports them can feel like insurmountable obstacles to change. "People don't change," we say. I think it's more that people don't take risks. I remember turning points in my life that required taking risks. The decision to follow Jesus as a young man took me down all sorts of crazy paths. It meant marrying quite young to start the spiritual journey of a lifetime. It meant choosing to proclaim my faith in baptism though this would result in being disowned from my family. It meant having more children than I thought I could handle and then adopting a child. It meant choosing to prioritize my family over career and leaving a traditional career for international mission service. It meant getting involved in the messiness of life and opening our home to strangers and friends. Looking back at all these choices still scares me. What was I thinking!? And why do I keep doing it?! In my case, I had an amazing wife who was willing to take the risks with me, but in some ways, this only heightened my fear of failing because I didn't want to fail her. But I made the choices nonetheless.

In retrospect, I can see how these choices challenged me, matured me, and changed me—and not just me, but us as a couple as well. But I had to get out of the chair and take some risks. There's a steep learning curve to get to the point of being able to enjoy what we have been given as human beings, created in the image of God. Unless you are willing to act, you will not change. Feeling a little insecure about it is a good thing. Change follows the actions you take. It rarely comes before.

Go back to some of the ideas that sparked your interest in Part 2, and pick one or two. Make some choices, take some small risks, engage a spouse or a friend in walking with you (literally and metaphorically), engage in some creative discussions, and you will gradually enjoy the changes it brings.

Stay well-resourced

It's a hot day, you're lined up on the marathon starting line, carbo loaded, loosened up, warmed up, and ready to go, except for one thing ... you forgot your water bottle. Despite all that preparation, you won't make it very far. The last component needed for integrating your design with the spiritual enhancements offered by Jesus are the resources that sustain you on the journey. Enduring the hardships and staying in it for the long haul require refreshment and nourishment along the way. Life is a marathon not a sprint, as they say.

I have found three main resources to keep me going for the long haul. The first is the presence of Jesus himself. I already pointed out that Jesus gives us His Spirit as a gift. There is no greater spiritual nourishment than that of the Holy Spirit. Jesus likened it to "eating His flesh." I know it sounds repulsive to our ears, but the point is that we can share the substance of life with Jesus, the Creator of life. He provides sustaining nourishment like the food we take in every day. The connection with Him can be real and sustaining if we stay spiritually alert.

Second, life is sustained by and within a community of faith. Seeing the presence of Jesus in others and in the work they do encourages and strengthens me to do the same. Hearing and discussing the words of the Bible—in the context of the story it tells—expand my vision and affirm my hope. Sharing with others in the worship, prayers, and personal sacrifices that reveal Jesus to the world builds my confidence that the story we all gather to tell has roots that go deep into our souls. As we discussed, this community may or may not be found in churches, but we must seek it out. It's sometimes found in the most unexpected places.

The third resource may come as a surprise. It may sound old-fashioned, but traditions are an important means to sustain our energy and direction. For example, in our home, we played the "no baby, no Christmas" game. As Christmas decorations were being set up, my wife would hide the baby Jesus figure from our crèche scene somewhere in our family room. No one got to open their presents until someone found the baby! There were some desperate moments, but we all had faith that the baby would be found. This tradition is a reminder that celebrating Christmas is not about the gifts or the decorations; it's about the story of Jesus' birth!

Use traditions to tell the story you really want your life to tell. My wife is the master at this. She tells stories with events and decorations, not just words (though she is good at that, too, by the way). On the day before Thanksgiving, we tell the story of life before conveniences by going without running water, electricity, or processed food of any sort. It reminds us to be thankful on

Thanksgiving. At Easter we put out Resurrection dioramas and do a Resurrection Easter egg hunt that tells the story of Jesus. We demonstrate how much we value each other by making personalized birthday cakes, giving thoughtful presents, and preparing favorite meals. We demonstrate the value of home by sharing traditional home cooking, putting out seasonal décor, and by keeping our home safe, clean, and orderly. We demonstrate the value of nature by gardening and camping. These are not old, stale repetitions of activities that mean nothing. Each tradition nourishes and sustains values that we want to hold in common for a lifetime.

Perhaps you could take some time this week with your community of faith to reimagine home and church traditions to more intentionally tell the story of a loving Designer. Take time to raise questions that increase spiritual awareness. We can each do our part to make sure we do a better job representing the story we want to tell.

For those of you wanting to enjoy the spiritual enhancements offered by Jesus, we must get our brains turned on, take some risks, and stay well resourced. It takes some effort, but with a little trial and error, a little time, and some patience, you will find the resources the Creator has provided are just what you need for the journey of a lifetime.

Glenn Strauss, M.D.

Chapter 22

Our divine design is just what this world needs

We started our journey with a poem I wrote that I think captures the ideas of this book well.

The Path Home

By G.H. Strauss

There are myths that hold us captive,
Stories that set us free;
There are tasks that bring us home
To rest in what we're designed to be.
Broken pieces of creation,
Partial truths of our design;
As shadows transformed to living wholeness
In the Presence of Light Divine.

It took a lot of words to get here, but it boils down to a few simple ideas:

Human beings exist in the middle of a mess of our own making. We are given a design as human beings that is just what this world needs to overflow with love and meaning, but it's hidden under layers of self-deception and ego. We uncover the hidden resources by visualizing ourselves as an integral part of the story of the Creator, designed to reflect His character and nature, and given tangible hope in a love story that will not disappoint us. We remain flawed, but by faith, we are spiritually gifted to embrace the fullness of our design and anticipate immortality with hope. Humanity is the center of the Creator's story, and He is ours.

It's a love story

I think what makes all this so attractive is the fact that it's a love story. You can call it a myth or a fable or even a delusion, and I can call it the truth, but, in the end, we are drawn towards it as our eyes are drawn to a light in the darkness. I could offer all sorts of evidence and arguments about the truth of the story told through the life and words of Jesus. But in the end, I think we respond because we all know a love story when we hear one. It's in our best interest and in our nature to prefer love over an impersonal story of fate or technology.

The stories of the followers of Jesus after He was physically gone demonstrate this love so well. These stories portray the mutual love between the Creator and His human partners. We see lives of ordinary people connected with Jesus in a loving embrace. It turns out that the best use of our divine design is in a loving partnership with others and with the divine Designer. We can limit ourselves to our basic design and favor other impersonal stories about who we are and why we are here, but why not embrace the story based on a loving Creator?

Learning to live by faith, not by "truth"

There is a lot hanging in the balance here. As rational and spiritual human beings, we are designed for faith and the pursuit of truth. We are in peril of losing part of ourselves if we pursue one without the other. Most of you reading this book grew up in a culture that values the quest for truth rather than the pursuit of faith. This leaves us at quite a disadvantage when it comes to experiencing the wholeness of life.

Even the "faith" community is often more about truth than faith. For example, when we say defenders of the faith, we usually mean defenders of the truth, as defined by various church doctrinal statements. There's nothing wrong with that per se, but unfortunately, we fool ourselves into thinking that these truths can be reduced to bumper stickers—pithy sayings that show we've got it all figured out. I'm embarrassed to say that Christians are particularly bad about doing this. We have the tendency to believe that if we put enough Bible verses on our refrigerator, we will become better people. If only it were that easy!

The reality is, we have to keep aligning ourselves with a story that we cannot prove, a Creator we cannot see, a design we cannot even fully understand, and an unseen spiritual realm that fills all of creation like some kind of alternate dimension. In short, we must learn to live by faith, not by "truth." We have no other choice. We don't need truth to help us find faith; we need faith to help us find truth. Jesus repeats this many times to His doubting followers.

Jesus offered His followers a story, not a doctrinal position. He claimed to be "the Way, the Truth, and the Life" but not in a reductive, doctrinal sense; His message and the events of His life showed the way, the truth, and the life in the expansive sense of a great story. His was THE great story to tell. Without the context of this story, we are only stacking truths together like a house of cards that keeps falling until we get it "just right." Faith is not like that. It holds us together in the uncertainty of life.

There is no need to despair! Jesus has invited us to live by faith, not by having it all figured out. The priceless gifts He gives make this possible. These gifts can be ignored or fought over but cannot be purchased or forced from His hand. We find wholeness in these gifts by accepting them as part of our own stories.

Where do you go from here?

I hope I have convinced you of two things: First, you must embrace the importance of being human. Second, if you are to become all you are designed to be, you must learn to embrace Jesus, the Divine Designer. This book was written to help you process both challenges.

From here, the way forward does present some challenges. The world has not changed; your friends and family are still the same as they were before you read any of this. In many ways you are still the same, too! But I put a pebble in your shoe, and I hope it bothers you enough that you stop what you are doing long enough to do something about it. And if you stop even for a moment, I hope you find that a seed of faith has been planted.

Remember that a small seed can grow into a beautiful flower or even a towering tree—it just needs some nurturing and time. Discuss your ideas with others. Ask questions. Be upset about what you see and hear around you. Nourish your faith by joining others to explore the life and teachings of Jesus. I invite you to use my book *The Importance of Embracing Jesus* as a guide, or read other authors intent on connecting you with the incredible reality of a spiritual domain—present right here, right now.

Regardless of where you go from here, be proud to be a human being, made in the image of God. Always remember it is your gift and privilege, not your curse. Never give up to this world what the Creator has designed for this world! And may the Spirit of God guide and direct you on your journey.

PROUD

TO BE
HUMAN

Glenn Strauss, M.D.

Appendix 1

The Good News About Our World

God's Plan and Our Place in It – Unpacking Our Founding Story

Excerpts from *Finding the Way* **by Glenn Strauss, 2019**

1. The fall of mankind should have ended the creation story.

In the beginning, Adam and Eve were designed to bear their Creator's image as beings with physical bodies, a mind, and a soul. Mankind was the pinnacle of creation, the one creature designed to relate with his Creator who himself is a spiritual being. Mankind was designed to be the perfect partner in this new creation story. But Satan convinced Adam and Eve that God was withholding crucial information about good and evil, leaving them incomplete. You can read the story of the disaster in Genesis 3.

Once Adam and Eve had defied God to obtain the knowledge of evil, they recognized the evil of their own defiance. They immediately recognized that they were damaged by it, not completed. And they could no longer enjoy the pure goodness of God's presence. Spiritually, they were now lifeless and disconnected from their spiritual potential. In fact, all creation was tainted. Man had invited evil into the perfect world and into their

THE IMPORTANCE OF BEING HUMAN

own lives. This could have been the beginning of the story of mankind filling the earth with the goodness of God. Instead, the partnership with man abruptly ended and creation was ruined. Apparently, Satan had won. Seemingly, God would have to destroy His creation and start over, or simply give the whole thing over to Satan. But it was not within God's loving perfection to take a single destructive step towards His creation plan.

There would be severe consequences. But instead of ending the whole story, God ended only the Garden of Eden. Instead of annihilation, God cursed mankind and His good creation. The curse introduced limits on mankind's ability to relate to God and ended His dominion once enjoyed over the good creation (Genesis 3:16–19). Death entered the picture and the whole physical world fell into a cycle of corruption and decay (Romans 5:12–14). There was separation from God rather than fellowship.

This should have been the end of creation... but it wasn't. God loved the world He created and promised to restore what was broken so He could complete His work (Genesis 3:15). Instead of destroying it or turning it over to Satan, God planned to restore it all, in fact, complete it, just as He had planned from the beginning. He would not destroy it or start over. He would not give Satan the ultimate victory.

This is good news!

2. The earth should have self-destructed under the dominion of evil.

With all creation and humanity living under a curse from its Creator, and with Satan exerting authority over creation as his domain, it would seem all was lost. Indeed, there are two pivotal stories in the Bible in which mankind nearly self-destructs. In the first story (Genesis 7 and 8), evil was driving mankind to self-annihilation when God stepped in to stop the carnage by providing a way for Noah, his family, and even animals to survive a catastrophic flood. In the second story (Genesis 11:1–9), evil corrupted the survivors of the Flood. Instead of believing the promises of God (remember the rainbow, Genesis 9:9–17), they began devising their own solutions for survival. They were thriving in the world after the Flood. Convinced of their own abilities, they built a huge tower in the land called Shinar. This project was located just to the east of the location where, ironically, the ark designed by God had saved them from the Flood. This tower was designed to demonstrate their supremacy by lifting them high above the earth to the very heavens. God knew that the pursuit of human supremacy would not solve the problem of evil; it only delayed the inevitable self-destructive pattern that would soon follow their achievement. In fact, this was exactly the same pattern that led to the downfall of Lucifer and his expulsion from God's presence (Isaiah 14:12–14). Mankind was not filling and subduing the earth as God had designed them to do as His partners. This was an attempt by humanity to dominate it without Him. God chose to scatter mankind and make it impossible for them to succeed in their quest for supremacy. The city was abandoned and later called the city of Babel to commemorate how God confused their communication.

It is important to note that angelic beings such as Lucifer (also created by God) were never intended to be God's earthly partners

THE IMPORTANCE OF BEING HUMAN

(Hebrews 2:5–16)—only His servants and messengers. This is why God did not prepare a solution to restore Satan (remember he "sinned from the beginning," 1 John 3:8). God lovingly arranged the solution to restore man, since we were the ones designed to be coregents with Him over creation. And in an unforeseen twist, God would not directly use His supreme power to annihilate Satan. Instead, He would use Satan as part of His secret plan to provide the solution for mankind. As all creation would learn, evil would be defeated by using evil for good (Romans 8:31–39).

To prepare the way for His solution, God chose a man, Abraham, to build a new nation, the nation of Israel (Genesis 12–15). God promised that His plan would be revealed and delivered through this nation by their Messiah, who would defeat Satan, not by taking control, but by submitting to death. Throughout Israel's history, as ugly as it was, we see God using His power to restrain evil and use it for good. He gave His people the royal law (the Torah) and in so doing, revealed the need for the Messiah, who would willingly pay the price to restore mankind. Israel's laws and the proclamation of their prophets ensured the survival of a remnant of people who believed in God's plan and waited for the Messiah to come to deliver them from evil.

The earth should have self-destructed under the dominion of evil . . . but it didn't. Throughout history, God restrained evil and used it by His power. All the earth was waiting for the great reveal: God himself would enter the restoration story in an unexpected way as the solution. God restrained evil for our sake. This is good news, but the best news was yet to come!

3. The death of Jesus should have marked the defeat of God's plan.

The depth of God's plan was shrouded in mystery. Why did God not just destroy evil directly and finally? Until Jesus came, neither the spiritual realm nor God's own people could see the whole picture (Romans 11:25). The first secret to be revealed was that the Messiah was actually God Himself (Colossians 1:26–27) submitting His deity to the form of a human being (Philippians 2:5–11). The virgin birth of Jesus into the world affirmed once and for all that God saw His creation as good, despite all the evil that came through mankind. This was a pivotal piece of God's plan to restore humanity to the job for which it was created.

Satan, of course, tried to silence Jesus by tempting Him to abandon His mission, hardening the hearts of His own people to His message, and even inciting execution at their hands. Once again, it appeared Satan had won. But as a final revelation of God's wisdom, Jesus' sinless life, innocent death, and miraculous resurrection actually fulfilled the requirements for God's plan and defeated Satan at the spiritual level. Satan thought he had eliminated the threat, but instead ended up defeated and, in fact, was the weapon of his own defeat. The death of Jesus as the God-man, affirmed once and for all that only by submitting himself to the curse that He himself had made against His creation, could God free His creation from the curse (Romans 3:26). The curse of the cross Jesus died on was the plan all along. God used evil to provide the ultimate weapon for defeating evil (2 Thessalonians 2:1–16). With sin and death defeated, He would launch a new realm on earth defined by restoration of His relationship and partnership with humanity.

The death of Jesus should have marked the defeat of God's plan . . . but His resurrection from the dead marked the beginning of a new era in human existence. Evil was no longer simply restrained, it was defeated (1 Corinthians 15:55–57). And because evil was defeated, spiritual life and a return to our purpose as human beings was once again possible. This is incredibly good news for us now. But, there were two remaining problems: First, Jesus returned to His heavenly home after completing His work, leaving mankind seemingly without a leader. Second, mankind, even with new potential for spiritual life, was still deeply flawed and inadequate to complete the work.

4. The physical departure of Jesus from the earth should have ended the mission.

You might think that life after the resurrection of your leader would be pretty exciting. But talk was about grave robbery, not victory over death (Matthew 27:64–66). The small group of followers did not understand what happened, but they knew they were still in trouble with the authorities. To make matters worse, within weeks after His victory, those first followers watched as Jesus returned to His spiritual realm (Mark 16:14–20, Acts 1:9-11). They were sad. They were confused. They had seen God's love, but now it was gone. He was gone. Why didn't Jesus stay around physically to finish the job? He promised He would be with them always (Matthew 28:20), but what did this mean for them now? It's hard to believe that Jesus would just leave the delivery of God's plan in the hands of a few followers, most of whom at some point had doubted or even deserted Him. How could God's plan succeed when it had already failed in the hands of people so many times?

The answer is that something fundamental had changed. Jesus' victory opened the door to the possibility of spiritual life for humanity (John 1:4, John 3:15–16, John 5:24, John 6:47, John 10:10, John 10:28). By believing God's plan, anyone could now have spiritual life (Acts 14:27, Acts 20:21, Romans 5:1, Galatians 2:20, Galatians. 3:26). It was not reserved for a certain nation or select religious leaders. It was available to all of humanity for the asking. And as an exclamation point in this already incredible plan, God would deliver and secure this new spiritual life by imparting His own life-giving Spirit (John 5:21, 26; John 6:63; Acts 1:5, 8; Ephesians 1:13). This was not the human spirit coming back to life; it was the infusion and intertwining of the Spirit of God with the human spirit, producing a brand-new life (2 Corinthians 5:17). For those who believed, God and man were now inseparable, no longer estranged. We once again could display the image of God, which was built into us. This was God's complete design for humanity.

The good news of God's plan spread. Followers seemed almost compelled to gather together. The Spirit of God united strangers and foreigners, men and women, young and old, those with no religious background, idol worshippers, atheists, and those who lived their whole lives religiously. They were united in one Spirit (Ephesians 2:13–18), and it was very clear that they had more to offer the world together than individually. But the Spirit of God not only united them; He transformed them (Ephesians 1:3–10; 3:3–6; 5:32). The change was so profound that those who received this new life were called "sons of God," His spiritual "children," a new creation (Ephesians 1:5, Galatians 3:26, Romans 8:16, 1 John 3:2).

THE IMPORTANCE OF BEING HUMAN

What a privilege to be the actual spiritual brothers and sisters of Jesus (Hebrews 2:11,17). And as Paul so brilliantly communicated, these early followers began to see themselves as the very body of the risen Christ they followed, each with unique gifts and abilities to use for expanding their sphere of spiritual influence (1 Corinthians 12:12–27), creating a sort of spiritual "Kingdom." Against all odds, despite intentional efforts to stop it, and even the persecution of those who believed in it, this new "Kingdom" of diverse people grew by leaps and bounds as the mystery of God's plan was revealed by the Word of God and by the lives of those transformed by it. This was the very Kingdom that Jesus came to launch!

It turns out, Jesus' physical departure was just what was needed to move God's plan of restoration forward (John 16:7). Because Jesus physically left, God put the final solution within the lives of Jesus followers as a gift. Human beings, though weak and still dying, became vessels of new spiritual life, acting as if they themselves had been resurrected from the dead (2 Corinthians 3:17–18). In fact, Jesus was living within them (Galatians 2:20). These "children" would carry the Kingdom of God, hidden within them, wherever they went (Luke 17:20–21, Acts 1:8)!

The mission on earth should have ended when Jesus physically left us . . . But it was just getting started! Thanks to God's loving plan to impart His own Spirit as a gift to His followers, they were given spiritual life and united as God's own sons and daughters. Now He could use them as His agents to deliver His promised plan to transform the fallen world (Acts 1:8). God would complete what He had started. As Jesus promised, His followers indwelt by His

Spirit were now prepared to do more to expand the Kingdom than He ever could (John 14:12). After all, this was God's plan for humanity in the first place (Genesis 1:27–28)! Jesus did not need to take over our job for us. He enabled us to do the job for which we were created. This was unbelievably good news!

5. The imperfection of humanity should make spiritual partnership with God impossible.

Despite this great spiritual victory over Satan and the new life that resulted from the infusion of God's Spirit into His followers, it was clear that the world was not suddenly transformed. Nor were Jesus' followers. The potential was there, but God's plan did not provide a restart button, an automatic escape route, or instant transformation. To make matters worse, God's defeated enemy was still allowed access to His creation! Satan's dominion was ended, but his ability to influence and deceive was not (Ephesians 2:2, 1 Peter 5:8). There was still sin, death, and decay. It may seem totally wrong to us, but God clearly intended His earthly Kingdom to exist alongside a fallen world (Matthew 13:24–31, 1 Corinthians 2:12, 2 Corinthians 1:12).

In the middle of this mess, God did the most amazing thing. He called His children to be partners with Him in restoring the earth (Hebrews 2:6–18). He united them, He transformed them, and then He called them to be "partners with Him in a heavenly calling" (Hebrews 3:1, 9). It was never God's intention to do the work He had designed mankind to do with Him. Despite being damaged by the rebellion at the beginning of the story, His image was still present giving mankind value and purpose. So how could God partner with mankind filled with all their imperfections? How could this new spiritual Kingdom be effective if it was full of imperfect people?

A surprise answer

The answer is surprising. From the beginning, even in the Garden before mankind rebelled (Genesis 3:3), God based His partnership with mankind on faith, not perfection. Adam and Eve were sinless and innocent, but they still needed faith. God's plan for them to fill and have dominion over the earth as His image bearers and delegates was based on their ability to trust that what He asked them to do was in their best interest. Even as they walked with their Creator in the Garden, they needed faith that the best way to fulfil their role in the partnership, was to do what God said was best. But their faith failed, and they did not trust. First, they doubted, then they rebelled. Failure in the Garden was not just rebellion, it was a failure of faith. The history of the pivotal role of faith goes all the way back to the very first people and is even spelled out by the writer of Hebrews (Hebrews 11), starting with the children of Adam and Eve.

Followers of Jesus throughout history have been imperfect representatives at best. Despite all their potential, His followers struggle with self-centeredness, uncertainty, fear, and impurity. Some do fall away. But the wisdom of God's plan is that since He alone provided the solution for the curse, we need only have faith (Romans 3:21–26, Ephesians 2:8), the faith of a child as Jesus taught (Mark 10:13–16). This is all we need to participate in this plan as His partners. All we need to do is simply align ourselves with God's plan by believing this good news is true. This is so ridiculously simple; Paul even called it the mystery of faith (1 Timothy 3:9). It was never about how much we know (remember the temptation in the Garden, Genesis 2:16–17, 3:1–5). It has always been about preferring God's plan for His creation over all others.

Summary of our founding story:

In the beginning, God starts a story of divine-human partnership in a beautiful new universe. The rebellion of man against his Creator could have ended the whole story. Instead, God ends the Garden of Eden with a curse that separates Him from close fellowship with His creation. Cursed by its own Creator, mankind dies spiritually, and creation begins decaying. But God, as an expression of His sovereign power, restrains evil and preserves creation even though it is cursed and damaged. At the same time, as an expression of His loving character and nature, God sets the stage to defeat evil, end the rebellion, remove the curse, and complete His creative work.

God keeps His master plan for the completion of creation as a mystery, but finally reveals Himself as the final solution for restoration. He launches a new spiritual realm on earth through the death and resurrection of Jesus, His human-born Son. As Jesus returns home to

His spiritual realm, He releases His Spirit to all those who would simply believe and follow His plan of restoration, thus initiating a new era in His fallen world. In this new era, by the grace of God through faith, people are no longer doomed to be the agents of evil but instead are transformed into agents of good as His own sons and daughters. God now invites us to find the way from being His children to being true spiritual partners, using all the resources He provides that allow us to go beyond our physical abilities as humans to work in His spiritual Kingdom.

With the restoration of humanity and all creation assured by God's plan, we may now by faith serve as true partners with Him in His gracious plan, living in light of the promise that Jesus will be restored as the rightful Lord over a completed spiritual and earthly realm where we will live with Him forever.

Appendix 2
How to Start a Conversation that Grows a Community

Excerpt from *The Importance of Embracing Jesus*
by Glenn Strauss, 2023

Why are questions so important?

We are not very good at listening to each other. We are more interested in asserting our opinions or telling our stories than taking time to hear someone else's. Our bandwidth for genuine engagement is quite limited. It's hard to even convince someone that you do actually want to listen. It's almost as if you need some sort of "I'm listening" signal. I have found that sincere questions can be helpful tools for engaging with others.

Questions help us fill in gaps in our understanding. We ask simple who, what, where, when, and why questions to clarify, expand, and prioritize the information we need to make good decisions. We ask how things work to help us process the complexity of our world and overcome our limitations. We ask what if, why not, why here, and why now questions to explore areas of interest and develop new ideas.

The funny thing is, questions are not just tools; they also tell others a lot about you. When you ask someone to say more about something, it's usually because you have a specific interest. What you want to know reveals a bit of who you are, and by asking, you are helping the speaker know how to best engage with you to keep the conversation going. Thoughtful, respectful questions can provide the stimulus for the development of trust and mutual respect.

I would go so far as to say that sincere questions are at the heart of growing relationships. No doubt, trust and respect are critical, but relationships won't grow unless you engage in meaningful dialogue. You can't walk together unless you can talk together. My point here is that what you talk about is largely framed by questions about yourself, life, and the world. In a way, how you do friendships is always answering the question, "What sort of friend do you want to be?" How you behave, especially when no one is watching, is always answering, "What sort of person do you want to be?" These questions define us. These questions are at the heart of healthy, growing relationships.

I think it makes sense to get more intentional about asking questions. Many of our day-to-day conversations are casual and shallow, even impersonal. There's nothing wrong with that unless that's all you ever do. So how do we ask questions that encourage relationships? Most people feel a bit awkward asking too many questions—like you're intruding in someone else's business. And I agree, we need to be selective about what we ask. We cannot ask questions just to satisfy our personal curiosity, and you won't get very far asking questions someone has no interest in answering. I have found that the trick to relationship-building questions is learning to ask questions that others feel are worth answering. The problem is, how do we know what that is?

Asking questions that matter

If you want to grow a relationship, you must learn how to ask questions that matter. My observation is that these usually fall into two categories: questions that define a moment and questions that define a community. Let me describe what I have observed.

I am sure you can think of several defining moments in your life that hinged on a question. "Will you marry me?" "Will you take the job?" "Are you ready to be a father?" are a few that come to mind. These questions frame situations that require life-changing choices—choices that are hard to take back. But choices like these only define what you will do. Some defining moments are about who you will be. Will you give in to the temptation to lie, to cheat, to steal? Or will you listen to your conscience and be trustworthy and kind? The answer to these questions will define who you are. In relationships with others, we cannot tell someone what they need to do, but you can grow a relationship by being there to remind them of who they want to be.

In addition to questions that define us individually, there are questions that distinguish us corporately. What products can we deliver to be successful? What can we afford to do for our employees? How do we keep our volunteers happy? What activities can we do as a family that are within our means? But sometimes we face question that take us beyond what we do to how we will do it.

What sort of family do we want to be? What values do we want to represent? How do we want our organization to be perceived? How do we want our church to be known in this city? What business are we in? What makes us valuable as a company to our partners and our employees? As individual members of various organizations, we don't usually get to tell them what to do, but just like our personal relationships, we can grow whatever community we are in by reminding them of who they want to be.

Let me give you some specific guidelines that have helped me ask questions that matter.

How to ask questions that grow a relationship

We all have a variety of different relationships. Some are casual, some close, some are family, and some business. Relationships are important and they always require communication. How can we contribute to a healthy relationship? The fundamentals of honesty and respect are critical, but these alone do not grow relationships. For this, we need to learn how to ask questions that grow the relationship.

It may be as easy as dropping questions that express concern or caring into a casual conversation. For example, as you listen to someone talk about their recent vacation, ask what they valued the most about their time away. They may reply with an example of something they enjoyed, but remind them you are asking them what they valued. Or it may be sensing the pain of someone you bump into at the supermarket revealed by a few questions of concern. It often leads to prayer on aisle 10!

Here are a few simple rules to help you:

Glenn Strauss, M.D.

1. Find the right time and place for asking questions. Timing is everything!
2. Be respectful and considerate. Attitude matters!
3. Ask questions about what someone is saying about themselves and their activities that helps you understand them, not just their activities. Empathy connects you.
4. Be ready to honest answer questions about yourself. Humility encourages trust.

It doesn't take much to ask effective questions that stimulate growth.

How to ask questions that grow a community

We all have agendas when meeting with others. It may be for simple enjoyment or for achieving certain tasks. Sometimes we meet with others to solve problems; sometimes for personal support and growth; or it may just be for a sense of belonging. These are all good reasons to meet with others. Unfortunately, in our individualistic society we seem to have lost many of the skills needed to do community well. I think it's fair to say many of us are adept at staying hidden in plain sight while many others are skilled at taking control for themselves. Sadly, some church cultures are often prime examples of both. So how can we participate in communities in ways that contribute to their growth?

Each group has its own personality, strengths, and weaknesses, just like an individual. Awareness of this personality can help you fit in to offer what you do best. Shared interests, genuine concern even for strangers, and careful listening so you can reflect on stories you hear can be helpful to find your way in a new group. It always takes time.

Here are some simple rules to help you in a group setting:

1. Come with something to share.
2. Come ready to learn from others.
3. Come expecting to do a little work to discover something new.
4. Come with constructive observations, not complaining.

Not all groups may be a good fit for you, so don't worry about moving on if it's just not working. Just remember, in so far as it's up to you, if you act like a member of the group, you can generally be a member of the group.

The small group setting

Home groups or small community groups of 12 to 15 people are ideal settings in which to practice these communication skills. My wife and I have hosted dozens of home group studies over many years. I approach each group as unique. There is no cookie cutter formula for what will work. Sometimes we offer a light meal, sometimes not. Sometimes we discuss topics, sometimes we discuss the Bible. Our groups have included music teams, international eye teams, friends, family, churchgoers, and non-churchgoers. We love it when we see the group interacting together as a whole, in huddles, and one-on-one. We are encouraged when we see participants asking each other questions that really matter and sharing thoughts that make the experience meaningful and fun for everyone. Real dialogue is occurring and as a result, significant growth.

Most often, these groups started as a simple conversation with someone. And the conversations started by asking a few questions that mattered to them. Everything from a meeting with a group of guys from our neighborhood around the firepit to a neighborhood Bible study and a church home group can be traced back to this beginning. Remember: If we get intentional about why we are meeting together with others, it guides how we do it.

Sometimes we need questions that stir the imagination and dialogue that broadens our thinking. Sometimes we just need encouragement and relaxation. But we all need questions that ignite our critical thinking pathways. We all need questions to grow.

Acknowledgments

Thanks to the many readers and commentors who kept the effort to finish this book alive. Special thanks to Dr. Steven Arrowsmith for his friendship in our spiritual journey together over many years, for keeping me grounded in reality as I wrote this book, and for his many contributions to this writing and to my life. Thanks to my dear friend Pastor Art Hill, who encouraged me as he patiently read and reread my edits and suggested so many good changes; to Dr. Randy Randall for his friendship and the many discussions over breakfast to help me process what I was thinking; to my son Jonathan and his wife, Emalie, for helping me see this book could be useful to those just starting their walk with Jesus and for developing the concept for the Proud to be Human sign, and to my granddaughter, Alyssa, for her development of the "To Be" logo; and thanks to Johannes Smith for being a critical voice for honesty about spiritual things.

Thanks to Steve and Karen Morris for their encouragement and for suggesting Roaring Lambs Publishers—I hope it is the beginning of something powerful for the Kingdom. I also extend a special thanks to Karen Steinmann for her editing expertise.

Special thanks to Pauline and Brian Harris for their tireless work to help me clarify my message and for the use of their beautiful cover art photo.

And most importantly, thanks to my wife, Kim, for her boundless love and keen eye for simple details that has kept our work together grounded and honest for all these years.

About the Author

Dr. Strauss began pastoral work in 1980 and international medical work in 1986 serving as a consultant for both governmental and non-governmental international projects. With a primary interest in education and pastoral care, he developed innovative techniques to combine cross cultural spiritual formation with high quality surgical training.

In 2004, Dr. Strauss left his private practice and church ministry for full-time work as a volunteer on Mercy Ships performing thousands of cataract operations and training dozens of U.S. and international ophthalmologists. His development work resulted in a state-of-the-art surgical training simulator for developing nations, a companion published surgical textbook, and a cloud-based quality assurance tool for surgical outcome monitoring. For his work in medical education, in 2009, he was awarded the highest civilian honor, the National Order of Commander, by the president of Benin, Africa. In 2017 he received

The Albert Ueltschi Award for Simulation in Ophthalmology presented by the International Society for Manual Small Incision Cataract Surgery, and in 2019, was honored to receive the Christian Ophthalmology Society J. Lawton Smith Award for exemplary service.

Published Christian author (Finding the Way, 2019), bible teacher, and international trainer, he continues to work on training others in the art of transformative relationships. Ministries include the Strauss Medical Mentoring Project (for international training and discipling) and The Tyler Garden Oasis (for those in spiritual crisis). All work is supported through donations to their projects on the New Horizons Foundation web site.

Glenn Strauss, M.D.

 Roaring Lambs Publishing; Dallas, Texas

Made in the USA
Las Vegas, NV
08 September 2023

77247944R00138